AF349956

Altar

Peter Schneider / Rosa Schamal / Manuel Süess

Die Ordnung der kleinen Dinge

Eine Bricolage S. 4–23

The Order of Little Things

A bricolage pp. 24–43

Edition Patrick Frey No. 264

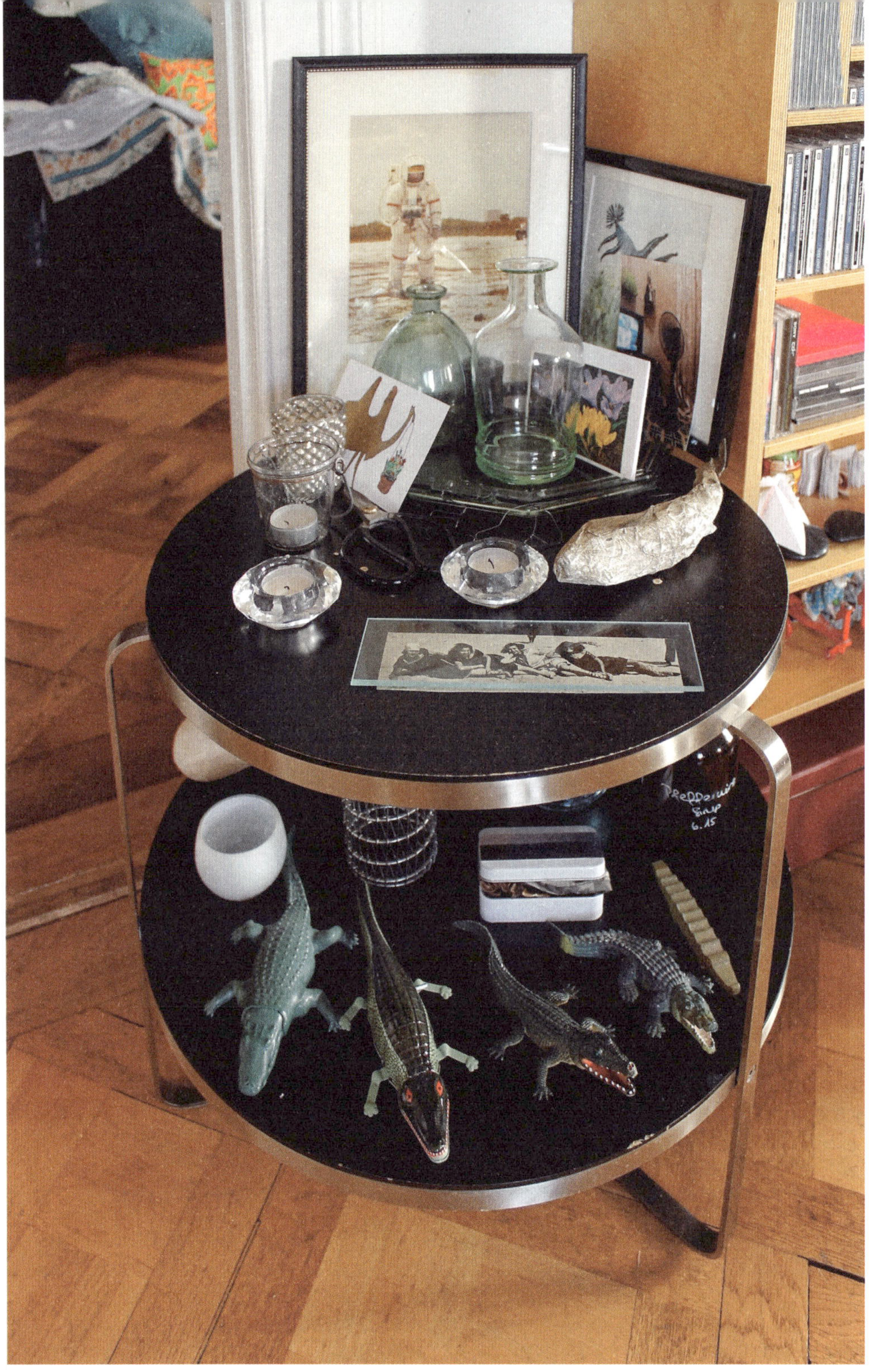

Die Ordnung der kleinen Dinge
Eine Bricolage

1 KUNST   Im Sommer 2016 besuchte ich die Ausstellung
The Keeper im New Museum an der Bowery in New York.
Diese Ausstellung, schreibt die Direktorin des Museums, Lisa
Phillips, in ihrem Vorwort zum Katalog, sei *«eine ungewöhn-
liche Ausstellung insofern, als sie die Funktion des Museums
multipliziert, indem sie [...] eine Vielzahl imaginärer Muse-
en und persönlicher Sammlungen zeigt — man könnte sie als
Museen des Individuellen betrachten».*[1]

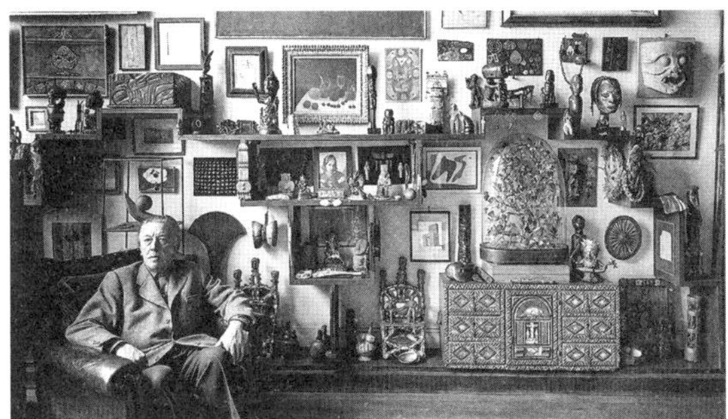

André Breton, Paris, 1955

Zwei der Künstler, die im New Museum zu sehen waren,
haben das Genre der Privataltäre zum Prinzip ihrer Arbeit
erhoben: der Brasilianer Arthur Bispo do Rosário (1909 – 1989)
und der 1956 in Japan geborene und seit 1980 in Brooklyn
lebende Yuji Agematsu.

In einem Interview mit Phon Bui, dem Herausgeber des
Kunstmagazins *The Brooklyn Rail*, beschreibt Agematsu den
Zusammenhang seiner Sammelkunst mit den Sammlungen
seiner Kindheit: *«Während des Sommers hing ich am Strand
herum und sammelte unter anderem Steine, Muscheln und
seltsames Seegras. Als ich ein Kind war, war Insektenjagen
eigentlich ziemlich beliebt. Die Kinder schufen Orte für sie.
Schmetterlinge, Ameisenlarven, Marienkäfer, Libellen, wir
sammelten alles.»* Später in New York erinnerte er sich wie-
der an seine frühen Interessen. *«Ich lief herum und sammelte diese Dinge, aber diesmal fand ich mich selbst. Jedes Mal,
wenn ich auf der Strasse ein Objekt fand, es aufhob und mir
anschaute, fand ich mich selber — wo ich hingehörte [...] es
gibt eine Verbindung zwischen dem, was ich von 1985 bis*

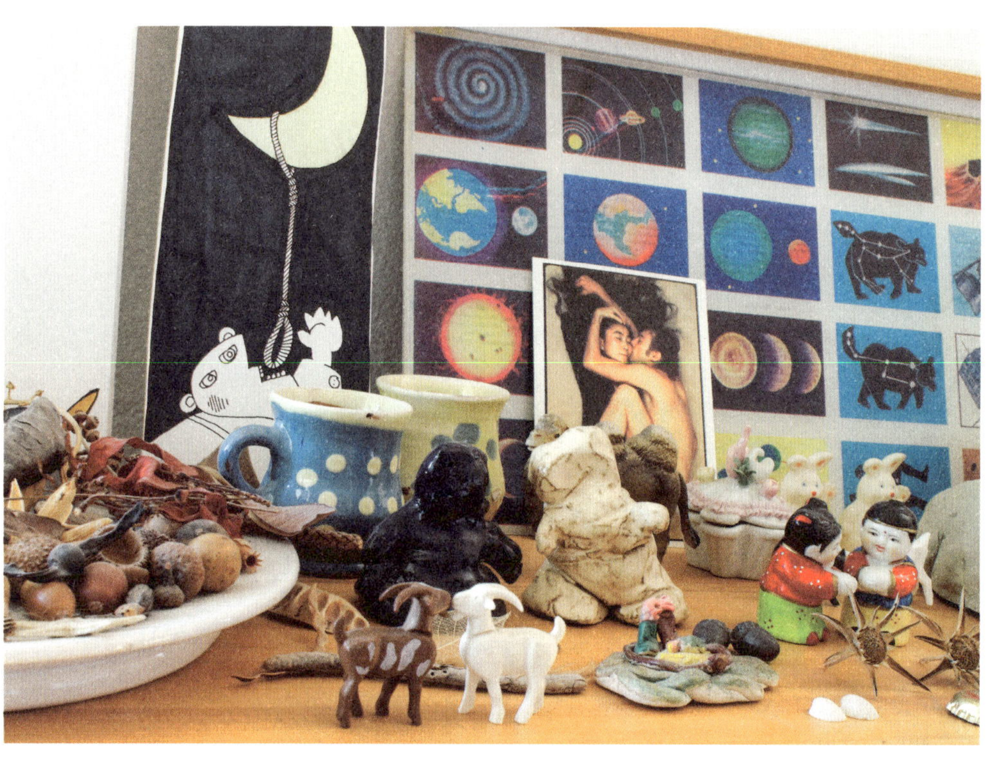

heute mache, und dem, was ich als Kind machte. Es fühlt sich wirklich so an, als ob ich all das schon seit meiner Geburt mache. Ich denke, dass jeder auf die gleiche Weise beginnt, Dinge zu berühren und aufzuheben. Es ist ein ganz normales menschliches Verhalten.»[2]

Agematsu vergleicht seine Sammlung von Gegenständen, die er in kleinen Cellophanhüllen wie in einem Terrarium präsentiert, mit musikalischen Kompositionen: *«Ich sehe Objekte als musikalische Notationen. Jedes Objekt hat seinen eigenen Klang und Rhythmus [...] ich sehe Objekte [...] als Personifizierungen. Ich dachte auch an die Beziehungen zwischen Subjekten und Objekten [...] Folglich dachte ich darüber nach, wie man den Betrachter zu den Objekten hinführen kann: indem man sie rhetorisch rahmt.»*

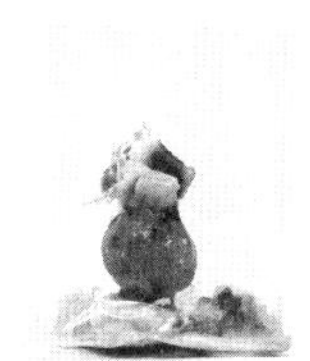

Yuji Agematsu,
ZIP: 01–01–14 – 12–31–14,
Portland, OR: Yale Union, 2015

Arthur Bispo do Rosário begann mit seiner Sammelkunst, nachdem ihm Engel erschienen waren, die ihn aufgefordert hatten, jedes Ding aufzubewahren, das es wert sei, am Jüngsten Tag gerettet zu werden. Seine Kunst ist eine Arche Noah der Dinge. Insgesamt stellte er während seiner Zeit in einer Irrenanstalt in Rio de Janeiro, in der er von 1938 bis zu seinem Tod 1989 wegen einer schizophrenen Psychose interniert war, fast 1000 Objektcollagen her.

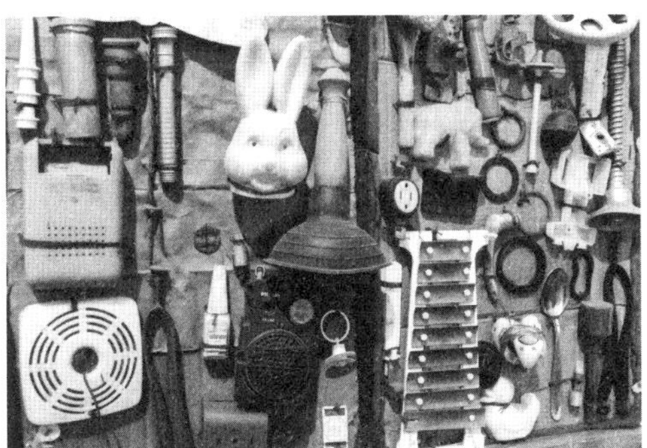

Arthur Bispo do Rosário, *The Keeper*, Installationsansicht / installation view, New Museum, New York, 2016

Seine Arbeiten sind Konkrete Poesie im wörtlichen Sinne, oder, um es mit zwei Termini Freuds zu sagen: eine Rückverwandlung von Wort- in Sachvorstellungen, ein Denken im Konkreten. In diesem Denken wird ein Rebus nicht nach seiner sprachlichen «Zeichenbeziehung», sondern nach seinem «Bilderwert» gelesen.[3]

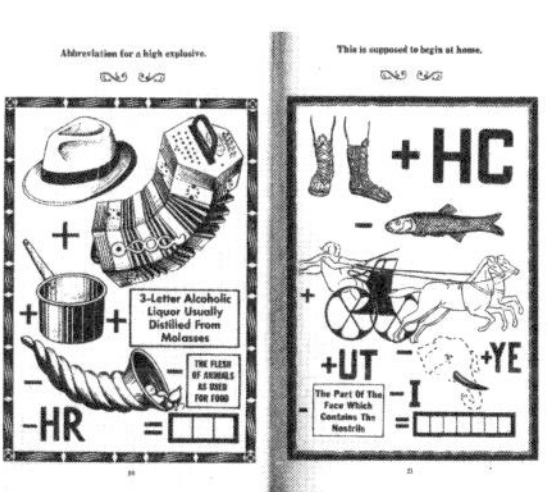

Everything's a Puzzle,
New York: Unicorn Books Inc., 1953

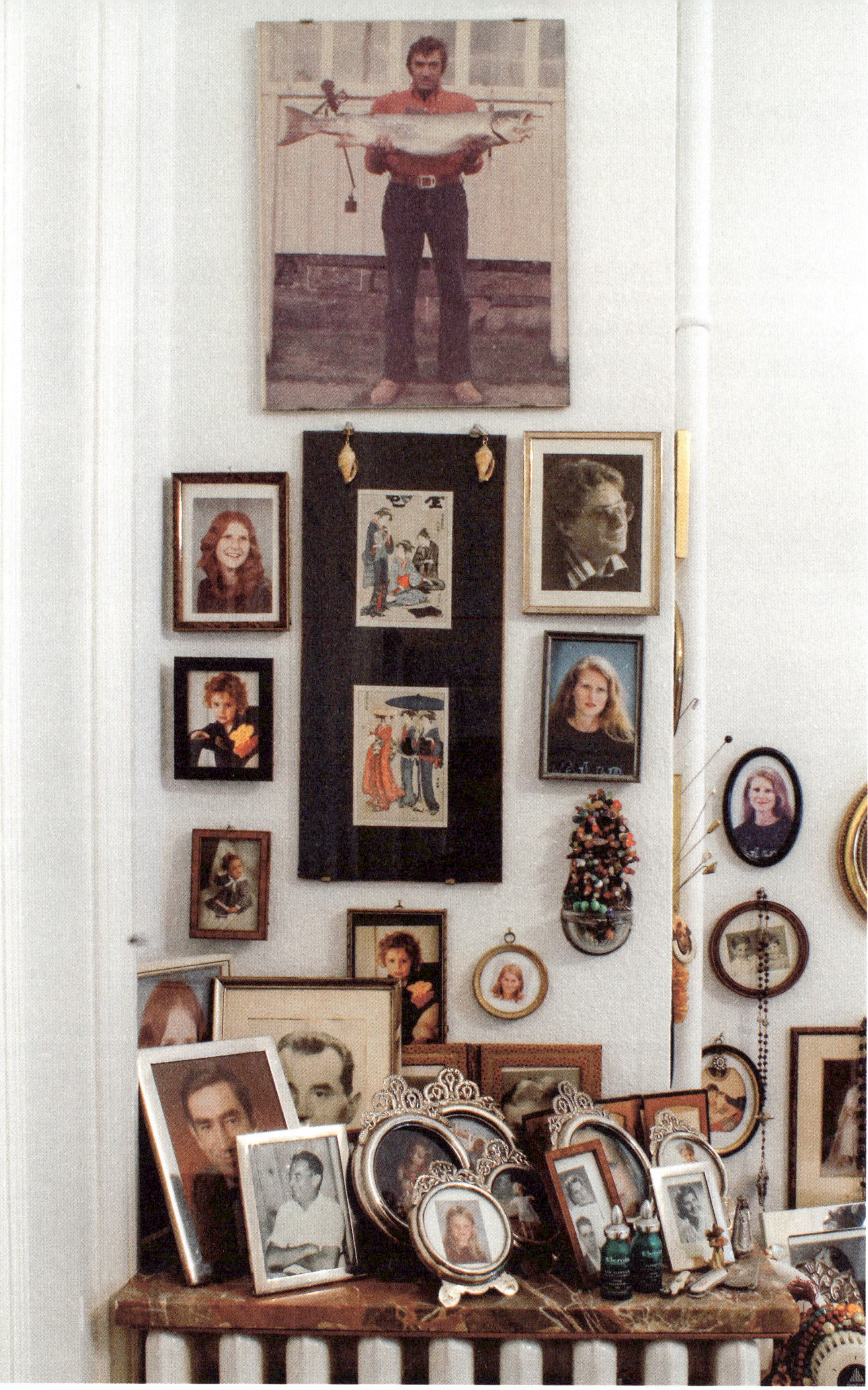

Darin kehrt ein Verhältnis zu Dingen als wissenschaftlichen Gegenständen zurück, das Lorraine Daston und Katharine Park in ihrem Buch *Wunder und die Ordnung der Natur* (2003) (Originaltitel: *Wonders and the Order of Nature*) beschrieben haben. Nicht das Gewöhnliche, Regelmässige, sondern das Wundersame, Aussergewöhnliche war von Interesse.[4]

«Aus dieser erstaunlichen Perspektive war frühe moderne Wirklichkeit (als) sporadisch — sowohl zeitlich wie auch räumlich (gesehen worden), die Welt war gesprenkelt mit Inseln unsicher verknüpfter Einzelheiten …», wie es John Sutton in seiner Rezension der Untersuchung der beiden Autorinnen formuliert hat.[5] Arthur Bispo do Rosário gibt den Gegenständen des Alltags in deren Neu(an)ordnung den Charakter des Aussergewöhnlichen.

Damit verleiht es den Dingen den Wert, bis zum Jüngsten Tag aufbewahrt zu werden.

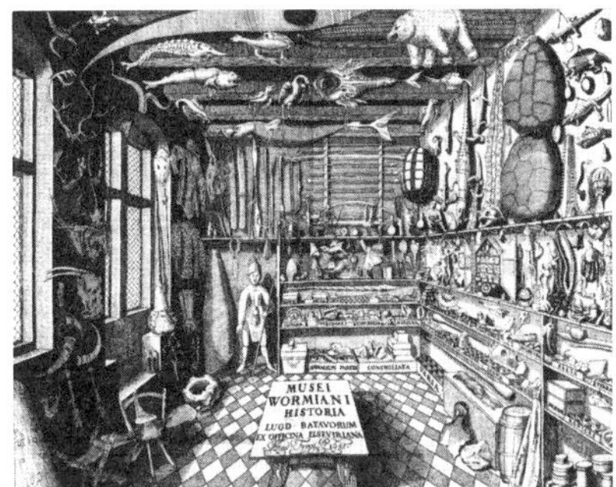

Ole Worm (Hg. / ed.), *Museum Wormianum,*
Amsterdam: Apud Ludovicum & Danielem Elzevirios, 1655

1 *Massimiliano Gioni und Natalie Bell (Hg.):* The Keeper. *New York: New Museum, 2016, S. 6.*

2 *http://brooklynrail.org/2017/05/art/Yuji-Agematsu-with-phong-bui*

3 *Siehe dazu Sigmund Freud: Gesammelte Werke. Frankfurt a. M.: Fischer, 1940ff., S. 283 f.: «Der Trauminhalt ist gleichsam in einer Bilderschrift gegeben, deren Zeichen einzeln in die Sprache der Traumgedanken zu übertragen sind. Man würde offenbar in die Irre geführt, wenn man diese Zeichen nach ihrem Bilderwert anstatt nach ihrer Zeichenbeziehung lesen wollte. Ich habe etwa ein Bilderrätsel (Rebus) vor mir: ein Haus, auf dessen Dach ein Boot zu sehen ist, dann ein einzelner Buchstabe, dann eine laufende Figur, deren Kopf wegapostrophiert ist, u. dgl. Ich könnte nun in die Kritik verfallen, diese Zusammenstellung und deren Bestandteile für unsinnig zu erklären. Ein Boot gehört nicht auf das Dach eines Hauses, und eine Person ohne Kopf kann nicht laufen; auch ist die Person grösser als das Haus, und wenn das Ganze eine Landschaft darstellen soll, so fügen sich die einzelnen Buchstaben nicht ein, die ja in freier Natur nicht vorkommen. Die richtige Beurteilung des Rebus ergibt sich offenbar erst dann, wenn ich gegen das Ganze und die Einzelheiten desselben keine solchen Einsprüche erhebe, sondern mich bemühe, jedes Bild durch eine Silbe oder ein Wort zu ersetzen, das nach irgendwelcher Beziehung durch das Bild darstellbar ist. Die Worte, die sich so zusammenfinden, sind nicht mehr sinnlos, sondern können den schönsten und sinnreichsten Dichterspruch ergeben. Ein solches Bilderrätsel ist nun der Traum, und unsere Vorgänger auf dem Gebiete der Traumdeutung haben den Fehler begangen, den Rebus als zeichnerische Komposition zu beurteilen. Als solche erschien er ihnen unsinnig und wertlos.»*

4 *Lorraine Daston und Katherine Park:* Wonders and the Order of Nature. 1150–1750. *New York: Zone Books, 1998.*

5 *https://johnsuttondotnet.files.wordpress.com/2016/03/sutton_review_daston_park.pdf*

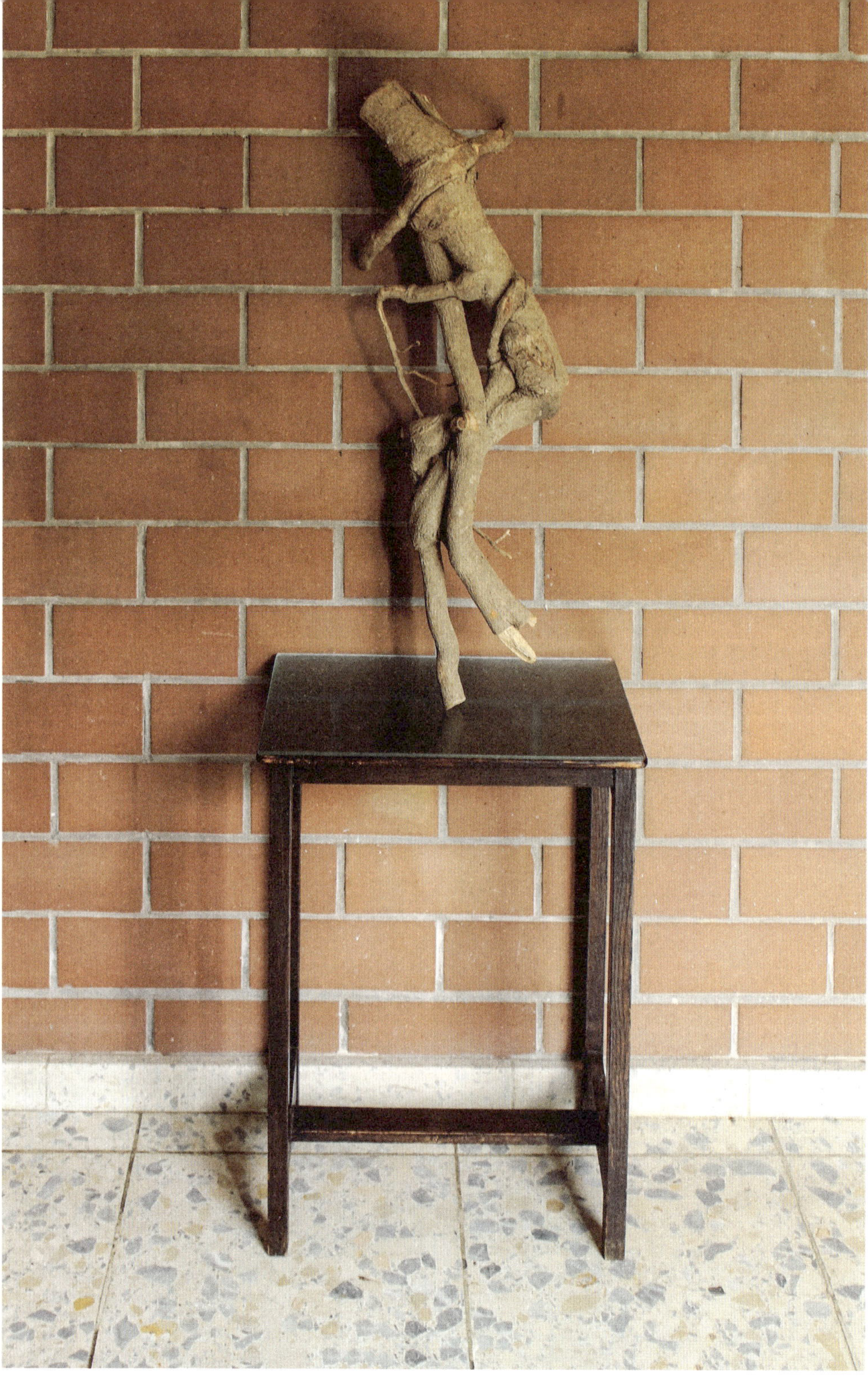

2 ORDNUNG   *«Die Dinge in meiner Umgebung lassen sich nicht klassifizieren»*, schreibt Vilém Flusser in der Einleitung seines Buches *Dinge und Undinge*, *«und zwar aus zwei verschiedenen Gründen. Erstens lassen alle möglichen Klassen eine Zahl von Dingen überhaupt aus, und zweitens gibt es Dinge, die bei jeder möglichen Klassifizierung unter mehr als eine Klasse fallen. Das ist ein äusserst unbefriedigendes Faktum. Denn wäre eine, oder mindestens einige, Klassifizierung der Umgebung möglich, dann könnte man sich darin orientieren. So aber kann man bestenfalls versuchen, sich nicht ganz darin zu verlieren.»*[6]

Die Ding-Collagen, diese Sammelsurien gleichförmiger oder auch völlig disparater Dinge, die Rosa Schamal «Privataltäre» nennt, umgehen Flussers Problem der Kategorisierung, indem sie, allein durch ihre Zusammenstellung, eine je eigene Kategorie, eine Privatkategorie, bilden. In *Die Ordnung der Dinge* zitiert Michel Foucault aus Jorge Luis Borges' Erzählung *«Die analytische Sprache John Wilkins»*, in der dieser wiederum «eine gewisse chinesische Enzyklopädie» zitiert, *«in der es heisst, dass ‹die Tiere sich wie folgt gruppieren: a) Tiere, die dem Kaiser gehören, b) einbalsamierte Tiere, c) gezähmte, d) Milchschweine, e) Sirenen, f) Fabeltiere, g) herrenlose Hunde, h) in diese Gruppierung gehörige, i) die sich wie Tolle gebärden, k) die mit einem ganz feinen Pinsel aus Kamelhaar gezeichnet sind, l) und so weiter, m) die den Wasserkrug zerbrochen haben, n) die von weitem wie Fliegen aussehen›»*.[7]

Diese kuriose Taxonomie der Tiere taugt offensichtlich nicht dazu, eine brauchbare Alternative zur tatsächlichen Kategorisierung der Tierwelt abzugeben. *«Was unmöglich ist, ist nicht die Nachbarschaft der Dinge, sondern der Platz selbst, an dem sie nebeneinandertreten könnten.»*[8]

Die Privataltäre schaffen einen solchen Raum. Ihre Ordnung ist identisch mit ihrer jeweiligen Anordnung, sie ist darum in keiner Weise zwingend. Anders als gewöhnliche Sammlungen sind die Ansammlungen von Dingen zwar auch jederzeit der Erweiterung fähig, aber sie bedürfen keiner Erweiterung. Sie sind von Beginn an gleichzeitig vollständig und ergänzungsfähig. Aber sie enthalten in sich kein verborgenes Prinzip, aus dem sich Anweisungen für eine Ergänzung ergeben würde.

Sie sind Schnappschüsse dinglicher Assoziationen.

6 *Vilém Flusser:* Dinge und Undinge. Phänomenologische Skizzen.
  Mit einem Nachwort von Florian Rötzer. München, Wien: Carl Hanser, 1993, S. 9.
7 *Michel Foucault:* Die Ordnung der Dinge. *Frankfurt a. M.: Suhrkamp, 1974, S. 17.*
8 *Ebd., S. 19.*

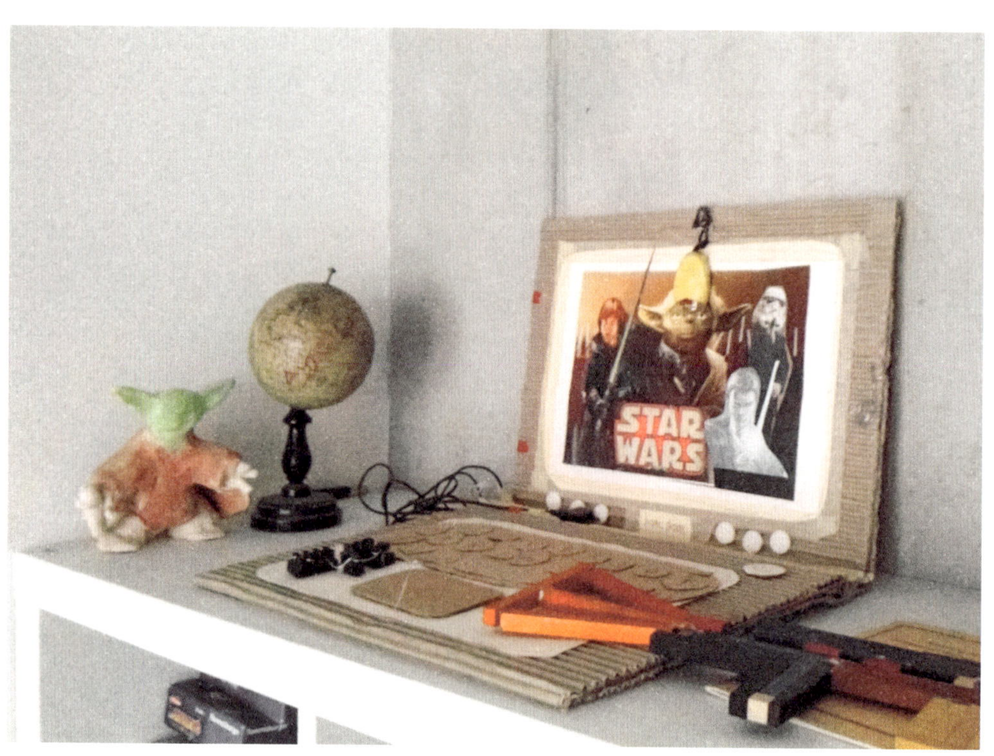

STAR
WARS

3 KINDER Die nächstliegende Analogie zu den Privat-
altären der Erwachsenen bilden die Sammlungen, die Kinder
in Zigarrenschachteln oder Keksdosen oder einem kleinen
Pappkoffer als Schatzkiste horten.

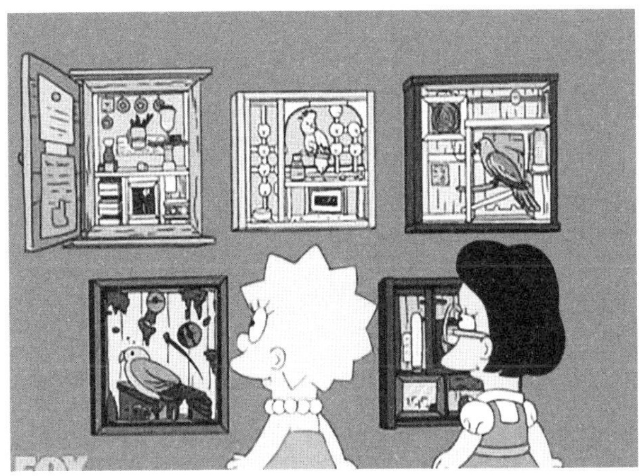

The Simpsons, «Die Chroniken von Equalia» / "Lisa the Drama Queen",
(Still), Staffel / season 20, Folge / episode 9

Darin sind selten Gegenstände, mit denen die Kinder
spielen, sondern vor allem Fundstücke, oft aus dem ursprünglichen Zusammenhang gerissene Gegenstände: ein verstei-
nerter Haifischzahn, eine Playmobilfigur, zwei Pokémon-
Karten, ein Kristall, ein kleiner Becher mit dem Bild der
Loreley …

In ihnen hallt weit entfernt die Tradition der Wunderkam-
mern nach. Sie enthalten keine Preziosen (jedenfalls nicht
im Sinne der Erwachsenen), aber «Dinge, die zählen» (Sherry Turkle), die auf ihre Weise und in anderen Gegenständen
ihre Bedeutung auch für das Leben des Erwachsenen behal-
ten. *«Wir sind es gewohnt, Objekte als brauchbar oder äs-
thetisch anzusehen, als Notwendigkeiten oder als nutzlosen
Genuss. Wenn wir Dinge als Gefährten unseres emotionalen
Lebens oder als gedankliche Anregungen betrachten, stehen
wir auf unsicherem Grund. Die Auffassung, dass inspirie-
rende Objekte* (evocative objects) *diese beiden weniger
vertrauten Vorstellungen zusammenbringen, unterstreicht
die Untrennbarkeit von Denken und Fühlen in unserer Beziehung zu Dingen. Wir denken mit den Objekten, die wir
lieben; wir lieben die Objekte, mit denen wir denken.»*[9]

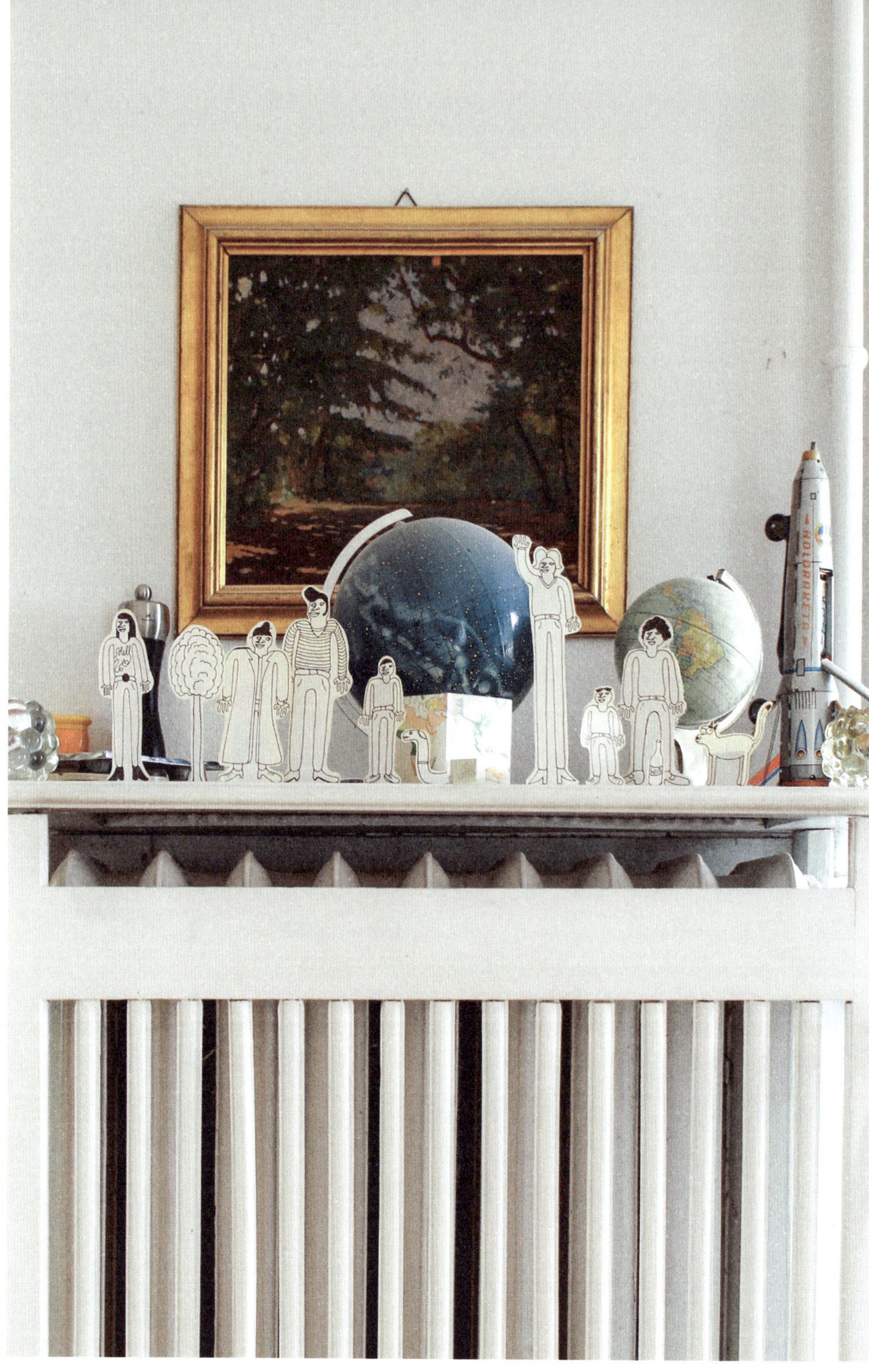
HOLDRAKÉTA

Die Dinge der Privataltäre verweisen nicht auf eine Ordnung
des Makrokosmos; ihre Anordnung bildet stattdessen einen
eigenen (selbstreferenziellen) Mikrokosmos. Wie die säku-
laren Hausaltäre (um bei diesem sakralen Begriff einmal zu
bleiben) der Erwachsenen lassen sich weder die Elemente
der kindlichen Sammelsurien noch das ganze Ensemble aus
der je einzelnen Funktion der in ihnen versammelten Gegenstände und in der Regel auch nicht durch eine erkennbare
Sammel-Maxime charakterisieren.

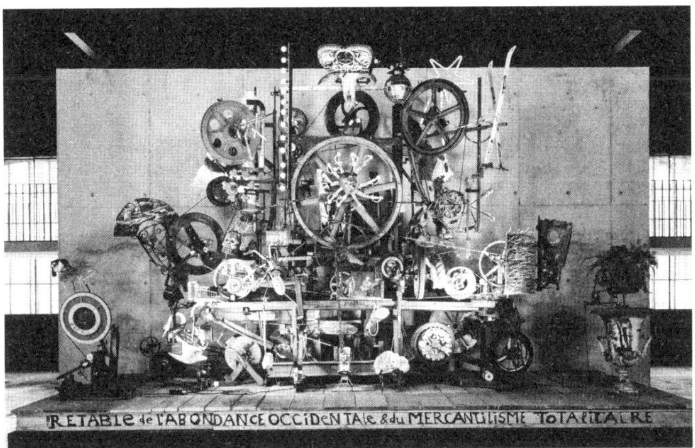

Jean Tinguely, *Altar des westlichen Überflusses und des totalitären Merkantilismus/
Altar of Western Affluence and Totalitarian Commercialism*, 1989/90

*«Kinderschätze können in der Regel nicht von Erwachsenen
erkannt und geschätzt werden»*, die Ignoranz der Erwachsenen ist die Chance der Kinder: *«In der Konsumgesellschaft
haben Kinder viel Besitz, der aber in der Nutzung reglemen-
tiert ist, und sie haben wenig Eigentum, über das sie wirklich
frei verfügen können. [...] Je weniger eine Sache für Erwach-
sene von Wert ist und je weniger eine Sache als Eigentum
einem Erwachsenen zugeordnet werden kann, desto eher
können sich Kinder diese Sache aneignen. Es sind so vor
allem die banalen, wertlosen Dinge, die zum eigentlichen
Eigentum von Kindern werden.»*[10]

Aber nicht nur die Kinder mit ihrem Krimskrams schlagen
der ökonomischen Wertehierarchie der Erwachsenen ein
Schnippchen. Auch die Dinge der Privataltäre zeichnen sich
oftmals dadurch aus, dass sie zu einer privaten Wertkate-
gorie gehören, die es beispielsweise möglich macht, sie
billig auf dem Flohmarkt zu erwerben.

9 *Sherry Turkle (Hg.):* Evocative Objects: Things We Think With. *Cambridge, MA: MIT Press, 2007, S. 5.*
10 *Burkhard Fuhs: «Der Zauber der Dinge in der Kindheit». In: Christina Schachtner (Hg.):* Kinder und Dinge.
Dingwelten zwischen Kinderzimmer und FabLabs. *Bielefeld: transcript, 2014, S. 80 und 81.*

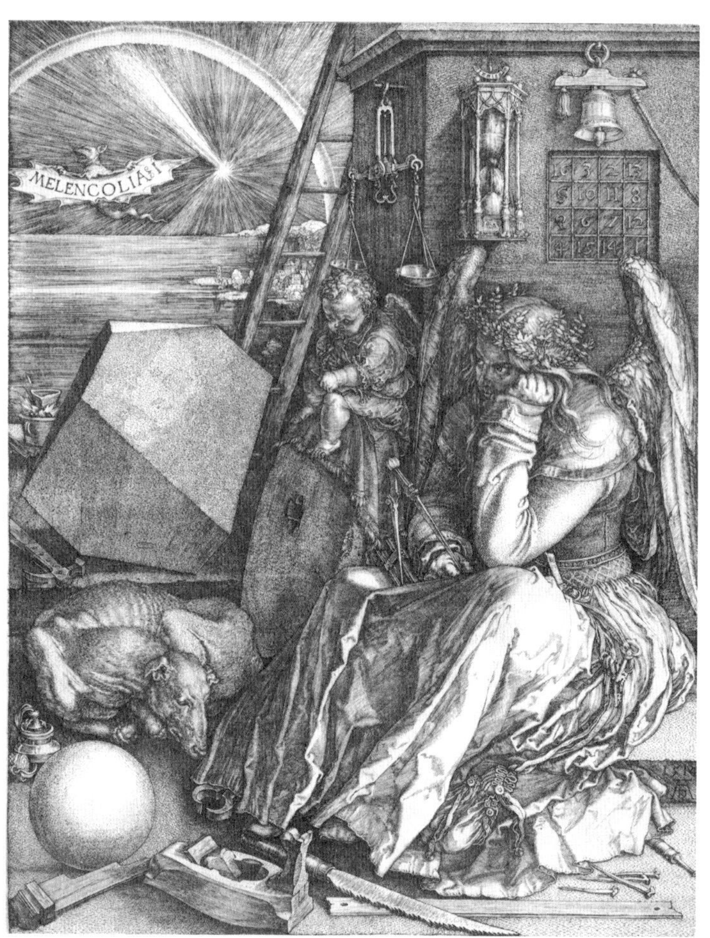

Albrecht Dürer, *Melencolia*, 1514

4 PATHOLOGIE Die Nischenökonomie der kindlichen Sammlungen, die private Wertehierarchie der Privataltäre hat ein
pathologisches Pendant in dem, was man im deutschen
Sprachraum seit den Achtzigerjahren gemeinhin «Messie-
Syndrom» nennt.

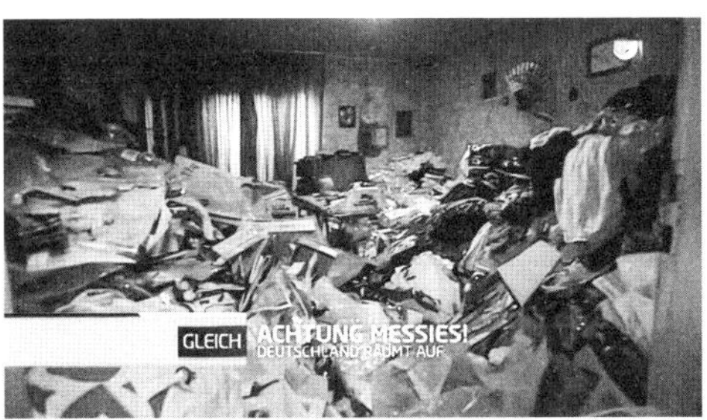

Achtung Messies! Deutschland räumt auf,
(Still), TV-Serie / TV series, DE 2011

Im Diagnosemanual DSM taucht es in dessen fünfter
Auflage erstmals als eigenes Störungsbild, der *compulsive
hoarding disorder*, auf. Das zwanghafte Horten ist ein be-
liebter Bestandteil des Unterhaltungsprogramms der Privat-
sender, die ihren Zuschauern regelmässig einen Blick in die
vermüllten Wohnungen ihrer Messie-Mitbürger gönnen. Als
alternativer Begriff für diese psychische Störung hat sich
auch der Begriff der «Wertbeimessungsstörung» etabliert.
Dem Messie geht die (ironische) Distanz ab, die der Schöpfer
der Privataltäre zu den von ihm aufgestellten Dingen bewahrt.

Die privaten Altäre sind zwar prinzipiell ergänzungsfähig,
aber sie haben keine Tendenz zu wuchern und mit dem anderen Hausrat zu einer einzigen Müllhalde zu verwachsen.

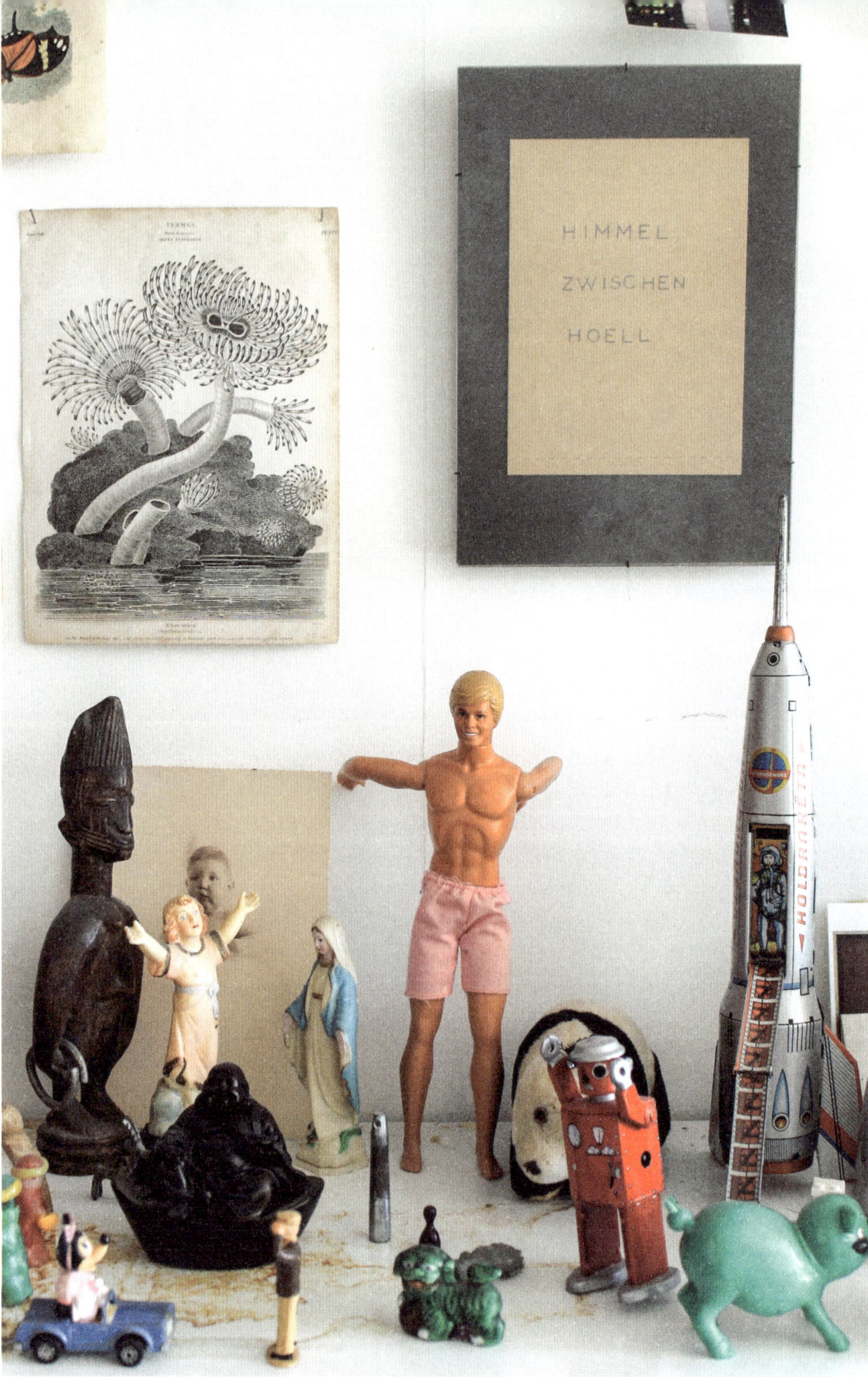
HIMMEL
ZWISCHEN
HOELL

5 POETIK   *The Comfort of Things* heisst ein Buch des britischen Anthropologen Daniel Miller, eine Feldstudie über die Bewohner einer Strasse im südlichen London.

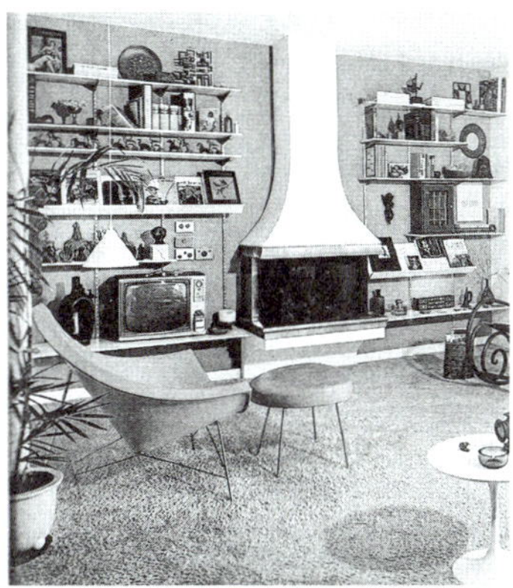

The Practical Encyclopedia of Good Decorating and Home Improvement, New York, NY: Greystone Press, 1970

«Was der Bewohner einer Wohnung oder eines Hauses über sich selbst, sein Leben und seine Beziehungen denkt, erfahren wir aus seinen Antworten auf unsere Fragen. Zugleich aber spiegeln sich seine Antworten und Erfahrungen in der Einrichtung der Zimmer wider, im Wandschmuck und den Teppichen, den Möbeln, die er ausgesucht und angeschafft, in den Kleidern, die er am Morgen angezogen hat. Das eine oder andere Stück hat er womöglich nur geschenkt bekommen oder geerbt — aber er hat es immerhin nicht weggeworfen, sondern in seine minimalistisch karge Wohnung oder sein bis unters Dach vollgestopftes Haus aufgenommen. Jedenfalls befinden sich die meisten Gegenstände nicht zufällig hier, sondern weil sie in irgendeiner Beziehung zum Bewohner des Haushalts stehen. Wenn es uns gelingt, diese Gegenstände zum Sprechen zu bringen, geben sie ein zweites, nicht weniger authentisches Statement ab.»[11]

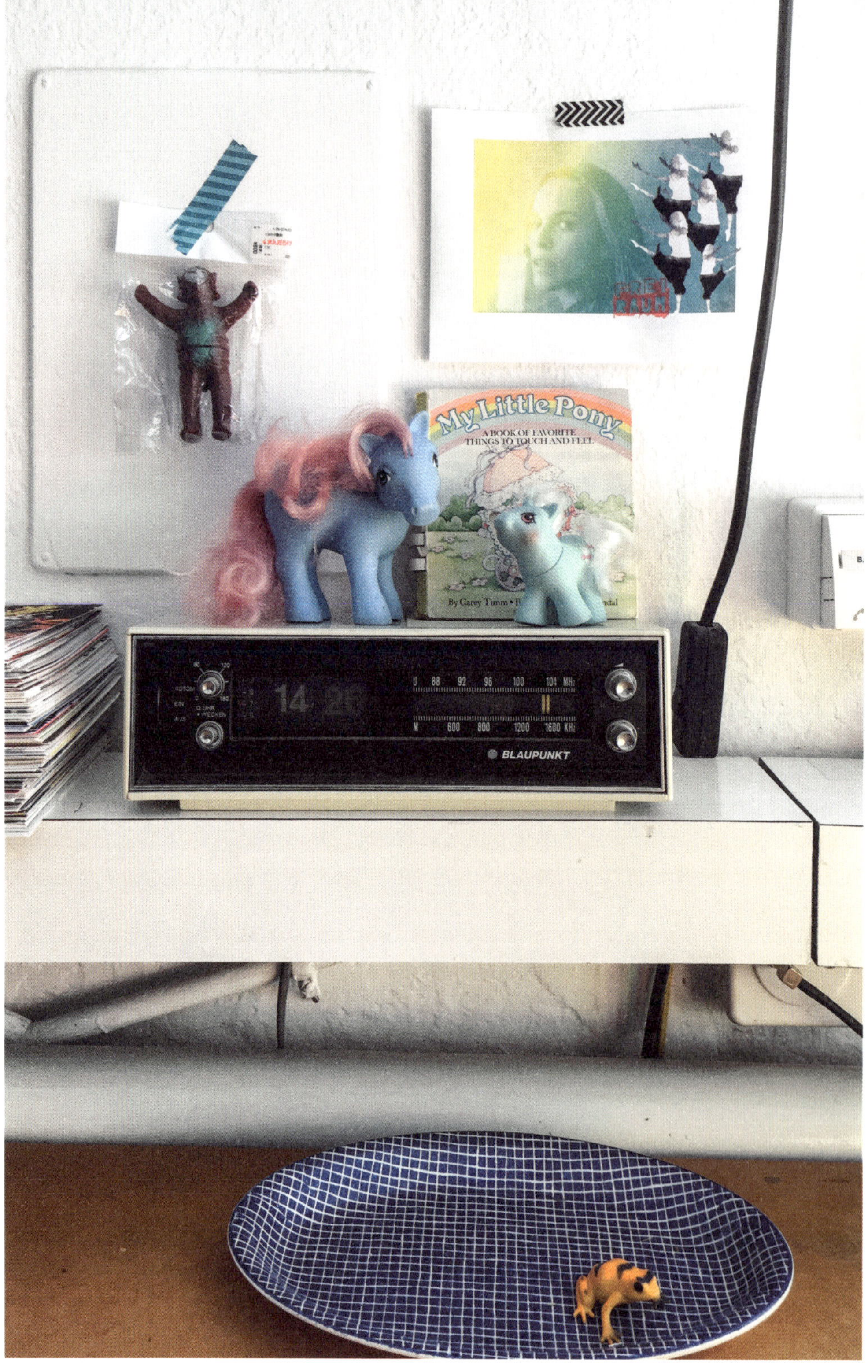

My Little Pony
A BOOK OF FAVORITE
THINGS TO TOUCH AND FEEL
By Carey Timm
BLAUPUNKT

Was immer die Dinge eines Haushalts zum Anthropologen sagen, sie sprechen Prosa wie ihre Besitzer. Sie verdoppeln, ergänzen oder konterkarieren das, was der Bewohner eines Haushalts sagt. Die Gegenstände, die in einem allfälligen Privataltar versammelt sind, sind durchaus Teil dieses Gemurmels der Dinge. Aber sie reden anders: «poetisch».

Nach Roman Jacobsons klassischer Definition der poetischen Funktion der Sprache projiziert diese *«das Prinzip der Äquivalenz von der Achse der Selektion auf die Achse der Kombination. Die Äquivalenz wird zum konstitutiven Verfahren der Sequenz erhoben.»*[12] Was in der geschriebenen oder gesprochenen Sprache sequenziell kombiniert wird, das wird bei den privaten Altären im Raum kombiniert, und zwar nach einem besonderen Äquivalenzprinzip, das nicht schon vorgängig in der Sprache existiert, sondern durch die Kombination erst geschaffen wird.

Private Altäre wirken darum als eine Art rätselhafter Poesie innerhalb der umgangssprachlichen Prosa der sonstigen Dinge.

11 *Daniel Miller:* The Comfort of Things (2008), *gekürzte deutsche Ausgabe:* Der Trost der Dinge. Berlin: Suhrkamp, 2010, S. 11.
12 *Roman Jacobson: «Linguistik und Poetik». In: Ders.:* Poetik. Ausgewählte Aufsätze. 1921–1971. *Hg. v. Elmar Holenstein und Tarcisius Schelbert. Frankfurt a. M.: Suhrkamp, 1979, S. 94.*

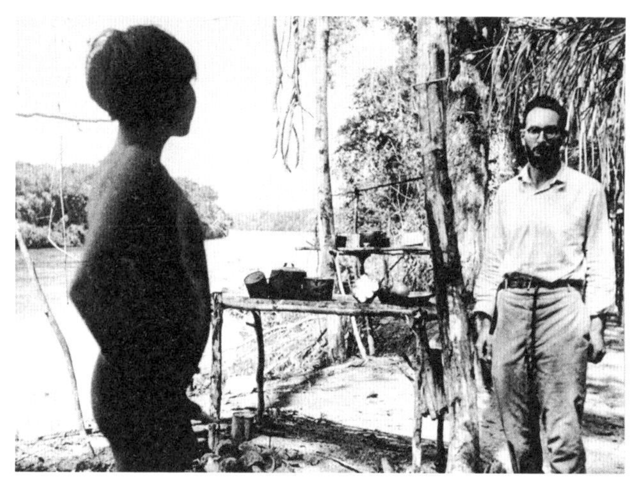

Claude Lévi-Strauss, Mato Grosso, ca. / c. 1935

6 BASTELN MIT LÉVI-STRAUSS *«Der Bastler ist in der Lage, eine grosse Anzahl verschiedenartigster Arbeiten auszuführen; doch im Unterschied zum Ingenieur macht er seine Arbeiten nicht davon abhängig, ob ihm die Rohstoffe oder Werkzeuge erreichbar sind, die je nach Projekt geplant und beschafft werden müssten: die Welt seiner Mittel ist begrenzt [...].*

Sehen wir ihm beim Arbeiten zu: Von seinem Vorhaben angespornt, ist sein erster praktischer Schritt dennoch retrospektiv: er muss auf eine bereits konstituierte Gesamtheit von Werkzeugen und Materialien zurückgreifen; eine Bestandsaufnahme machen oder eine schon vorhandene umarbeiten; schliesslich und vor allem muss er mit dieser Gesamtheit in eine Art Dialog treten, um die möglichen Antworten zu ermitteln, die sie auf das gestellte Problem zu geben vermag. Alle diese heterogenen Gegenstände, die seinen Schatz bilden, befragt er, um herauszubekommen, was jeder von ihnen ‹bedeuten› könnte. [...]

[...] die Signifikate werden zu Signifikanten und umgekehrt.

Diese Formel, die der Bastelei als Definition dienen könnte, erklärt, dass für die mythische Reflexion die Gesamtheit der verfügbaren Mittel gleichfalls implizit aufgenommen oder geplant werden muss, damit sich ein Ergebnis definieren lässt, das immer ein Kompromiss zwischen der Struktur des instrumentalen Ganzen und der des Projektes sein wird. Wenn dieses Projekt einmal verwirklicht ist, wird es also unvermeidlich gegenüber der ursprünglichen Absicht verschoben sein, ein Effekt, den die Surrealisten zutreffend ‹objektiven Zufall› genannt haben. Man kann aber noch weiter gehen: das Poetische der Bastelei kommt auch und besonders daher, dass sie sich nicht darauf beschränkt, etwas zu vollenden oder auszuführen; sie ‹spricht› nicht nur mit den Dingen, wie wir schon gezeigt haben, sondern auch mittels der Dinge: indem sie durch die Auswahl, die sie zwischen begrenzten Möglichkeiten trifft, über den Charakter und das Leben ihres Urhebers Aussagen macht. Der Bastler legt, ohne sein Projekt jemals auszufüllen, immer etwas von sich hinein.»[13]

13 *Claude Lévi-Strauss:* Das Wilde Denken, *Frankfurt a. M.: Suhrkamp, 1973.*

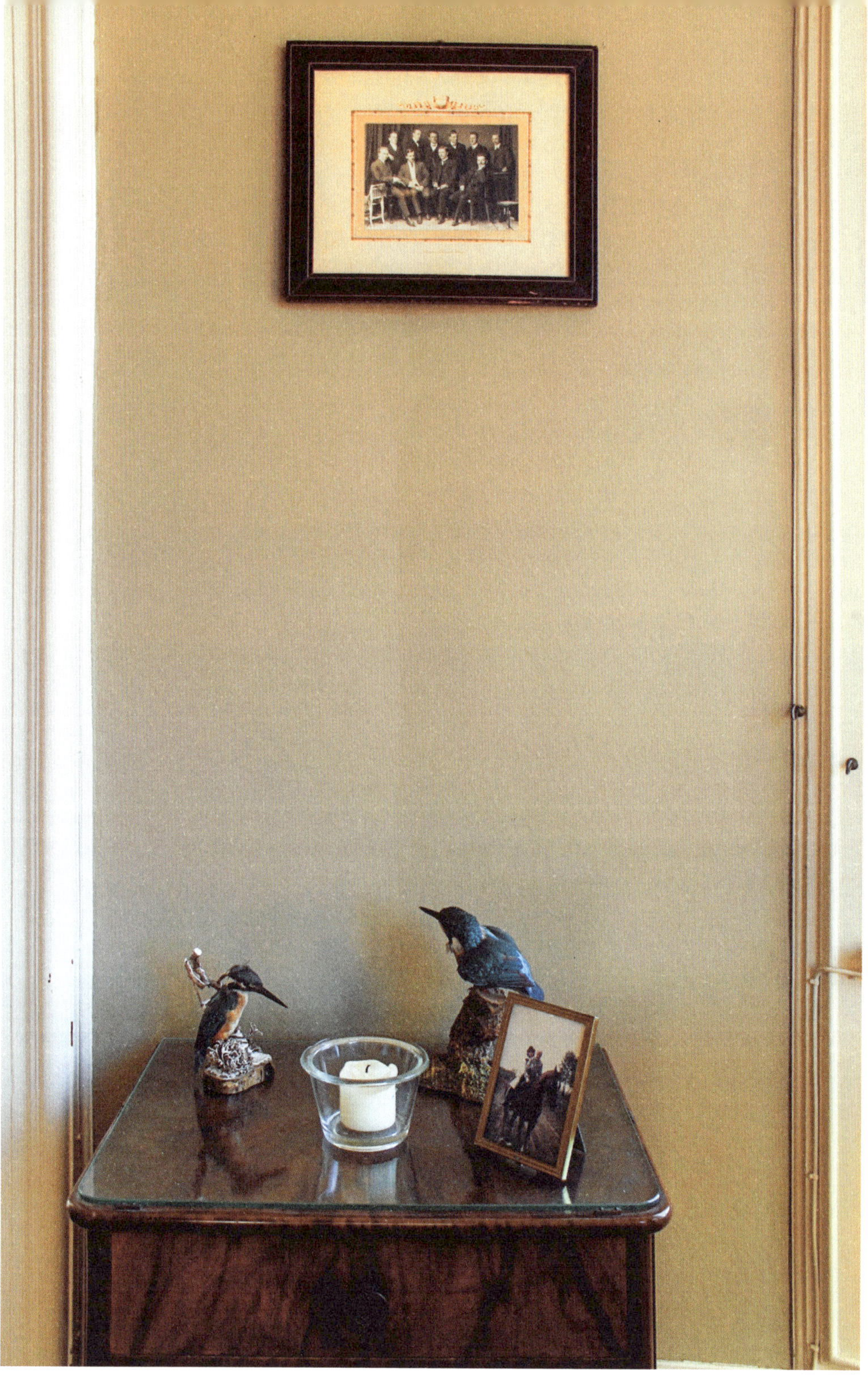

The Order of Little Things
A bricolage

1 ART   In the summer of 2016 I saw an exhibition at the New Museum on Bowery Street in New York called *The Keeper*. This show, writes museum director Lisa Phillips in her preface to the catalog, is *"an unusual exhibition in that it multiplies the function of the museum by presenting [...] an array of imaginary museums and personal collections — what one might consider to be museums of the individual."*[1]

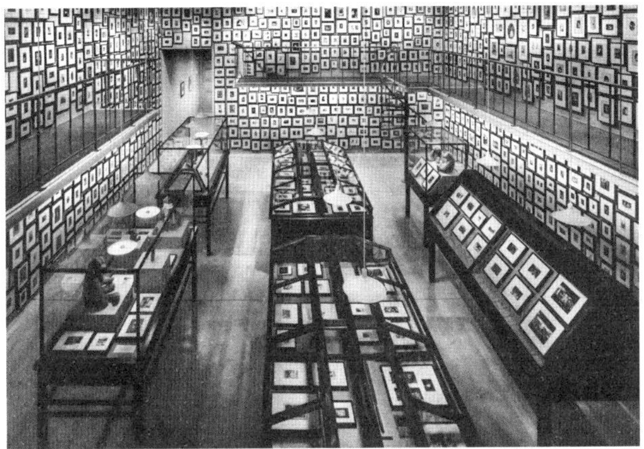

The Keeper, Ausstellungsansicht / exhibition view, New Museum, New York, 2016

Two of the artists featured there have clearly elevated private altars to an art form: the Brazilian Arthur Bispo do Rosário (1909 – 1989) and Yuji Agematsu, who was born in 1956 in Japan and has been based in Brooklyn since 1980.

In an interview with Phong Bui, cofounder and artistic director of the art magazine *The Brooklyn Rail*, Agematsu describes how the art of collecting ties into his childhood pastime: *"In the summertime I hung around the beach and collected stones, shells, and weird seaweed, among other things. Insect hunting was in fact really popular when I was a kid. Children would make spaces for them. Butterflies, antlions, ladybirds, dragonflies, we would collect everything."* Later on, after moving from Japan to New York, *"[...] my own original interests came back to me. I'd walk around and collect these objects, but this time I was finding myself. Each time I found an object on the street and picked it up to take a look at it, I was finding myself — where I belonged. [...]*

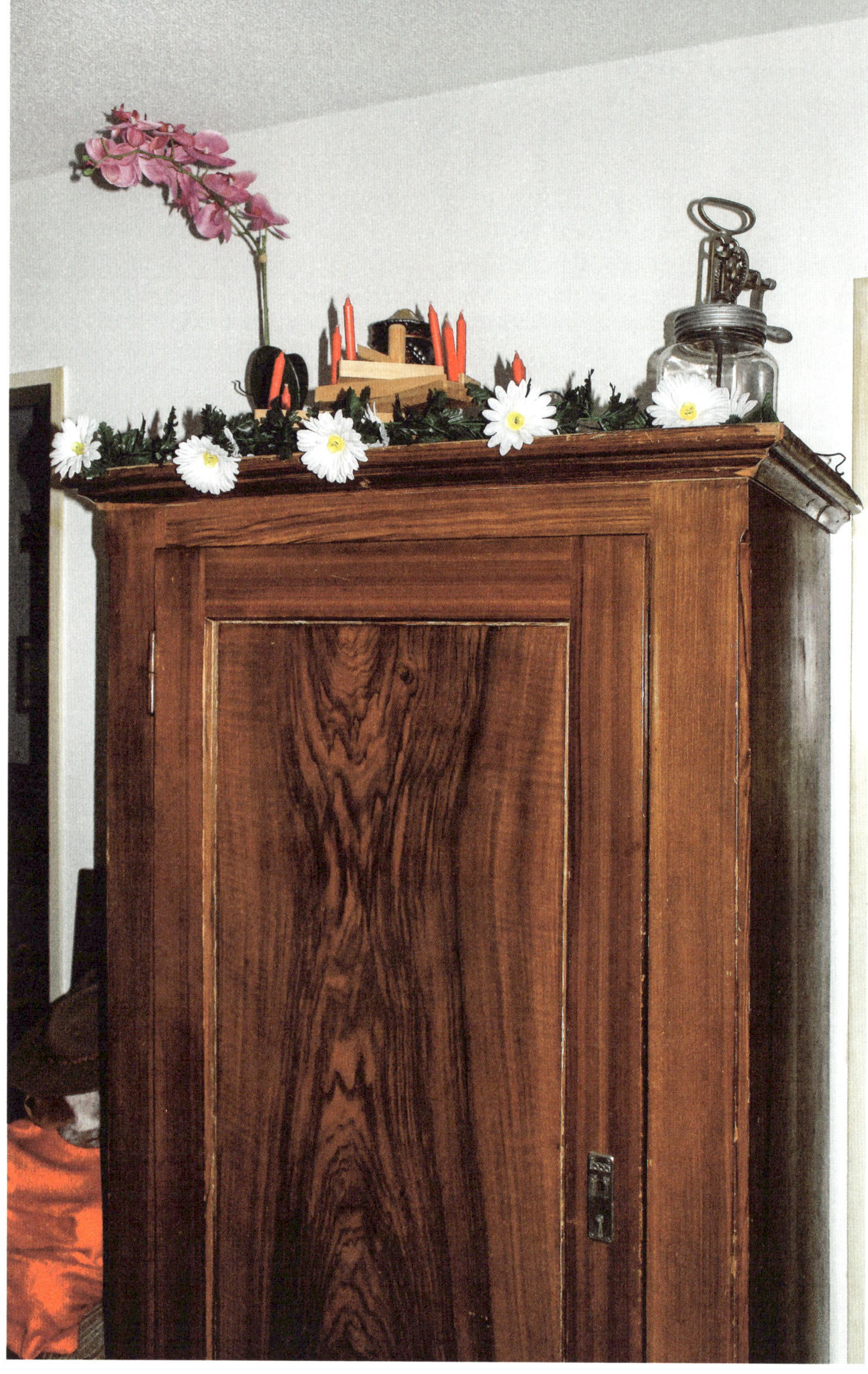

there's a connection between what I have been doing from 1985 until now, and what I did as a kid. I really feel as though I have been doing this since I was born. I think everybody starts with the same kind of touching and picking up of objects. It's just a normal human behavior."[2]

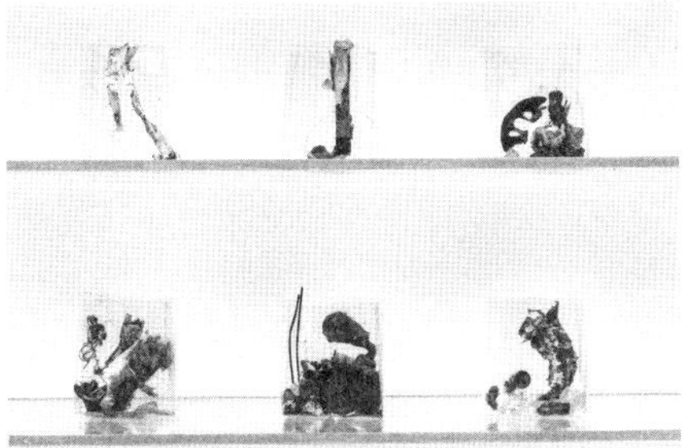

Yuji Agematsu, *Self-Portrait*, Miguel Abreu Gallery, New York, 2017

Agematsu compares his collection of objects, which he displays in small cellophane wrappers as in a terrarium, with musical compositions: *"I see each object as a notation in terms of music. Each has its own sound and rhythm. [...] I think of the objects [...] as personifications. I was also thinking of the relationships between subjects and objects [...]. So I thought about how to lead the viewer to the objects by using the rhetoric of framing."*

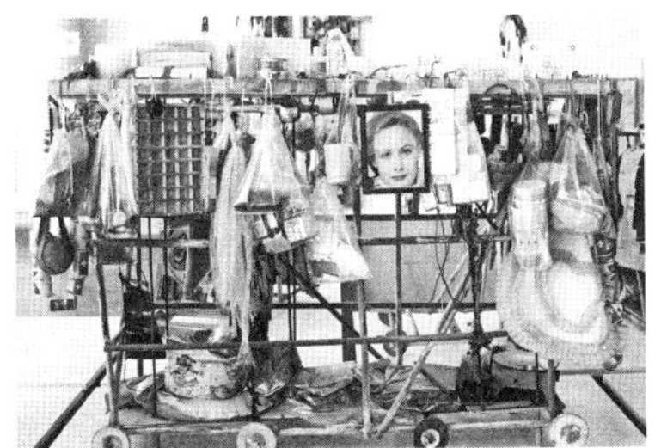

Arthur Bispo do Rosário, Installationsansicht / installation view, 30th Bienal de São Paulo, São Paulo, 2012

Arthur Bispo do Rosário began creating his *Sammelkunst* after angels appeared to him and told him to keep everything that was worth presenting to heaven on Judgment Day. His art is a kind of Noah's Ark of things. Diagnosed with schizophrenia at 29, he spent the remaining 50 years of his life, from 1938 till his death in 1989, in a psychiatric hospital in Rio de Janeiro, where he produced nearly a thousand collages of found objects.

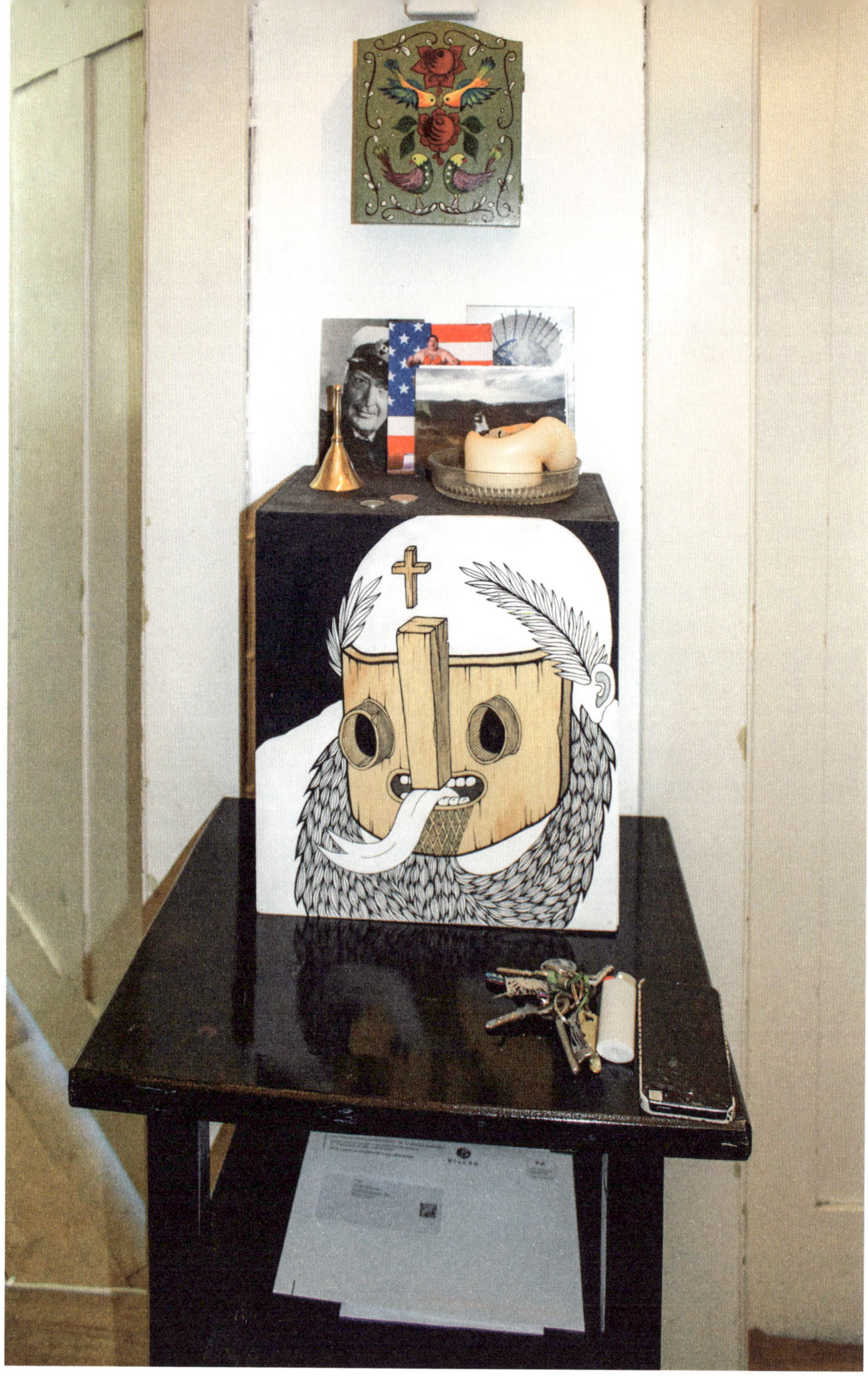

His works are concrete poetry taken literally, or in Freudian terms: a reconversion of "verbal ideas" *(Wortvorstellungen)* into representations of things *(Sachvorstellungen)*, a way of thinking concretely. In this concrete thinking, a rebus is read not according to its semantic "meaning as symbols" *(Freud's Zeichenbeziehung)*, but according to its "value as pictures" *(Bilderwert)*.

It involves a return to relating to things as scientific objects as described by Lorraine Daston and Katharine Park in their book *Wonders and the Order of Nature*. It is not ordinary, commonplace things that are of interest, but extraordinary wonders.

"On this striking perspective, early modern reality was (seen as) sporadic in both time and space, the world dotted with islands of uncertainly–related particulars," wrote John Sutton in his review of the author's study.

Bispo do Rosário endows everyday objects with the quality of the extraordinary in their new arrangement, their new order. Which in turn makes them worthy of being preserved until Judgment Day.

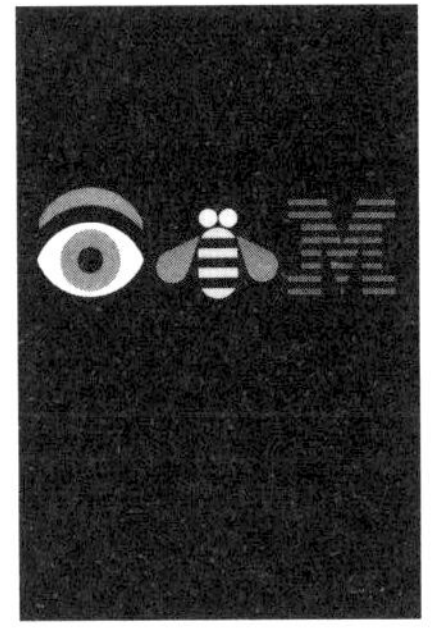

Paul Rand,
The rebus poster (IBM),
1981

1 *Massimiliano Gioni and Natalie Bell (Eds.):* The Keeper. *New York: New Museum, 2016, p. 6.*

2 *http://brooklynrail.org/2017/05/art/Yuji-Agematsu-with-phong-bui*

3 *See Sigmund Freud:* The Interpretation of Dreams. *Mineola, NY: Dover Publications, 2015, pp. 234–235: "The dream-content is, as it were, presented in hieroglyphics, whose symbols must be translated, one by one, into the language of the dream-thoughts. It would of course be incorrect to attempt to read these symbols in accordance with their values as pictures, instead of in accordance with their meaning as symbols. For instance, I have before me a picturepuzzle (rebus): a house, upon whose roof there is a boat; then a running figure whose head has been apostrophised away, and the like. I might now be tempted as a critic to consider this composition and its elements nonsensical. A boat does not belong on the roof of a house and a person without a head cannot run; the person, too, is larger than the house, and if the whole thing is to represent a landscape, the single letters of the alphabet do not fit into it, for of course they do not occur in pure nature. A correct judgment of the picture-puzzle results only if I make no such objections to the whole and its parts, but if, on the contrary, I take pains to replace each picture by the syllable or word which it is capable of representing by means of any sort of reference, the words which are thus brought together are no longer meaningless, but may constitute a most beautiful and sensible expression. Now the dream is a picture-puzzle of this sort, and our predecessors in the field of dream interpretation have made the mistake of judging the rebus as an artistic composition. As such it appears nonsensical and worthless."*

4 *Lorraine Daston and Katherine Park:* Wonders and the Order of Nature. 1150–1750. *New York: Zone Books, 1998.*

5 *https://johnsuttondotnet.files.wordpress.com/2016/03/sutton_review_daston_park.pdf*

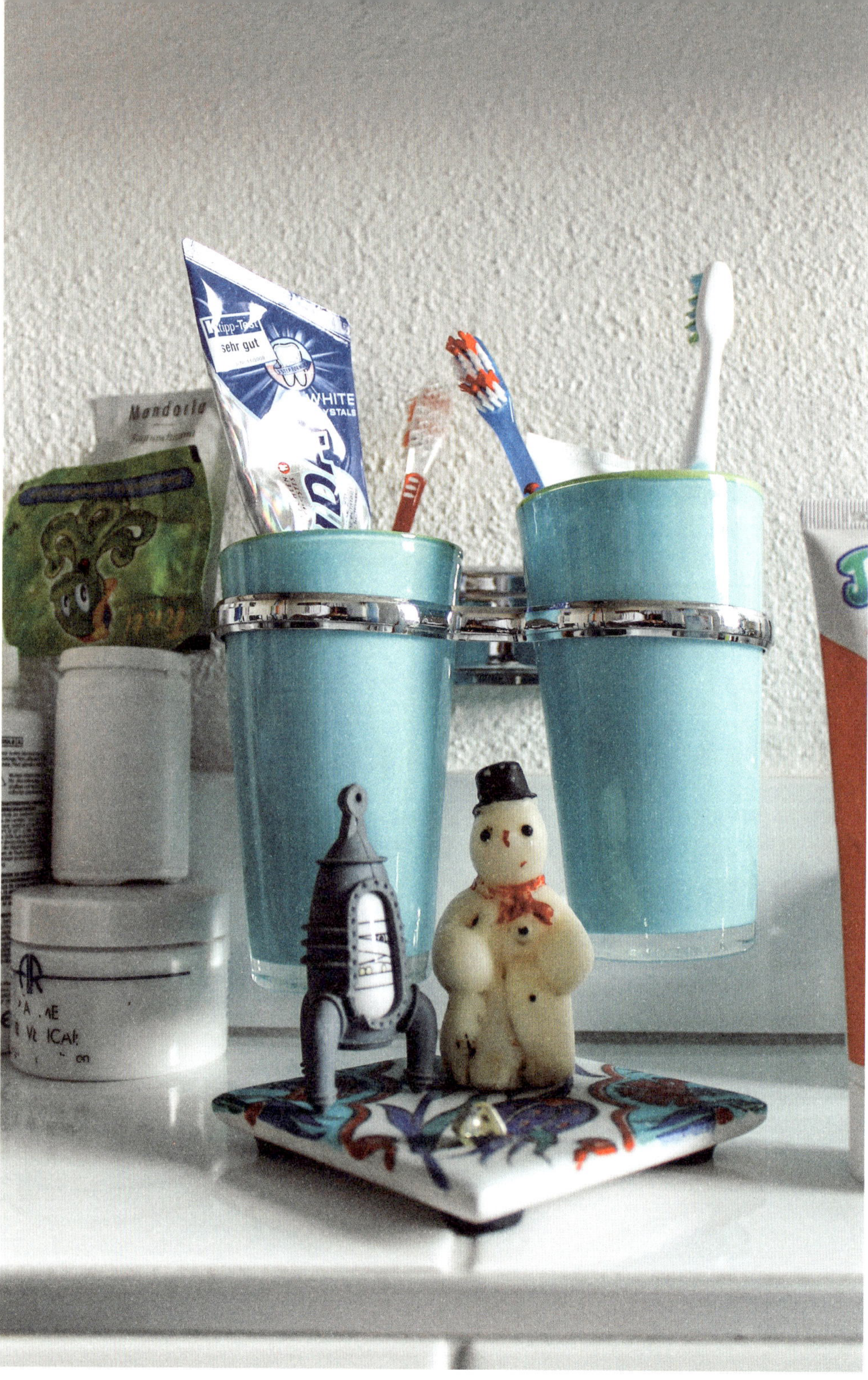

2 ORDER *"The things in my environment defy classification,"* writes Vilém Flusser in the introduction to his posthumously published book *Dinge und Undinge (The Shape of Things)*, *"[...] and for two different reasons. First of all, every possible class leaves a number of things out anyway, and secondly, there are things which, however they may be classified, will nonetheless fall into more than one class. This is an extremely unsatisfactory fact. If just one, or at least a few, classifications of our environment were possible, we could take our bearings by them. But as matters stand, the best we can do is try not to get completely lost in it."*[6]

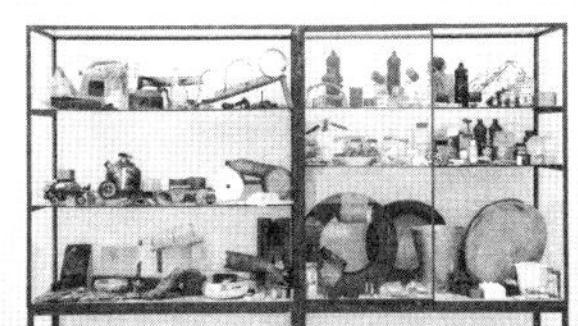

Alexander Calder & Fischli / Weiss, Installationsansicht / installation view, Fondation Beyeler, Riehen, 2016

These collages of things, these hodgepodges of similar or utterly disparate objects, these "private altars", sidestep Flusser's categorization problem inasmuch as each altar forms its own, private category. In *The Order of Things*, Michel Foucault quotes from Jorge Luis Borges' essay *"The Analytical Language of John Wilkins"*, in which Borges, for his part, quotes from "a certain Chinese encyclopaedia" in which it is written that *"animals are divided into: (a) belonging to the Emperor, (b) embalmed, (c) tame, (d) sucking pigs, (e) sirens, (f) fabulous, (g) stray dogs, (h) included in the present classification, (i) frenzied, (j) innumerable, (k) drawn with a very fine camelhair brush, (1) et cetera, (m) having just broken the water pitcher, (n) that from a long way off look like flies."*[7]

This curious taxonomy of animals clearly would not serve as a viable alternative to the scientific genus-and-species classification system. *"What is impossible is not the propinquity of the things listed, but the very site on which their propinquity would be possible."*[8]

Private altars, however, create just such a site. Their order is identical to their specific arrangement, hence by no means mandatory. Unlike ordinary collections, these assemblages can be supplemented at any time, to be sure, but they not need to be. From the outset, they are both complete and amenable to additions. However, they do not contain within themselves any hidden principle that might provide instructions for such additions.

They are snapshots of thing-based associations.

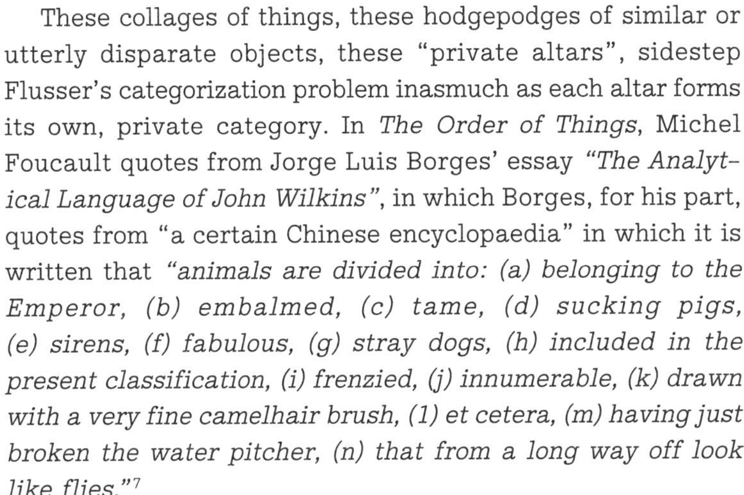

6 *Vilém Flusser:* Dinge und Undinge. Phänomenologische Skizzen.
   With a postscript by Florian Rötzer. Munich, Vienna: Carl Hanser, 1993, p. 9 (Our translation).
7 *Michel Foucault:* The Order of Things. *New York: Vintage Books, 1970, p. 17.*
8 *Ibid., p. 19.*

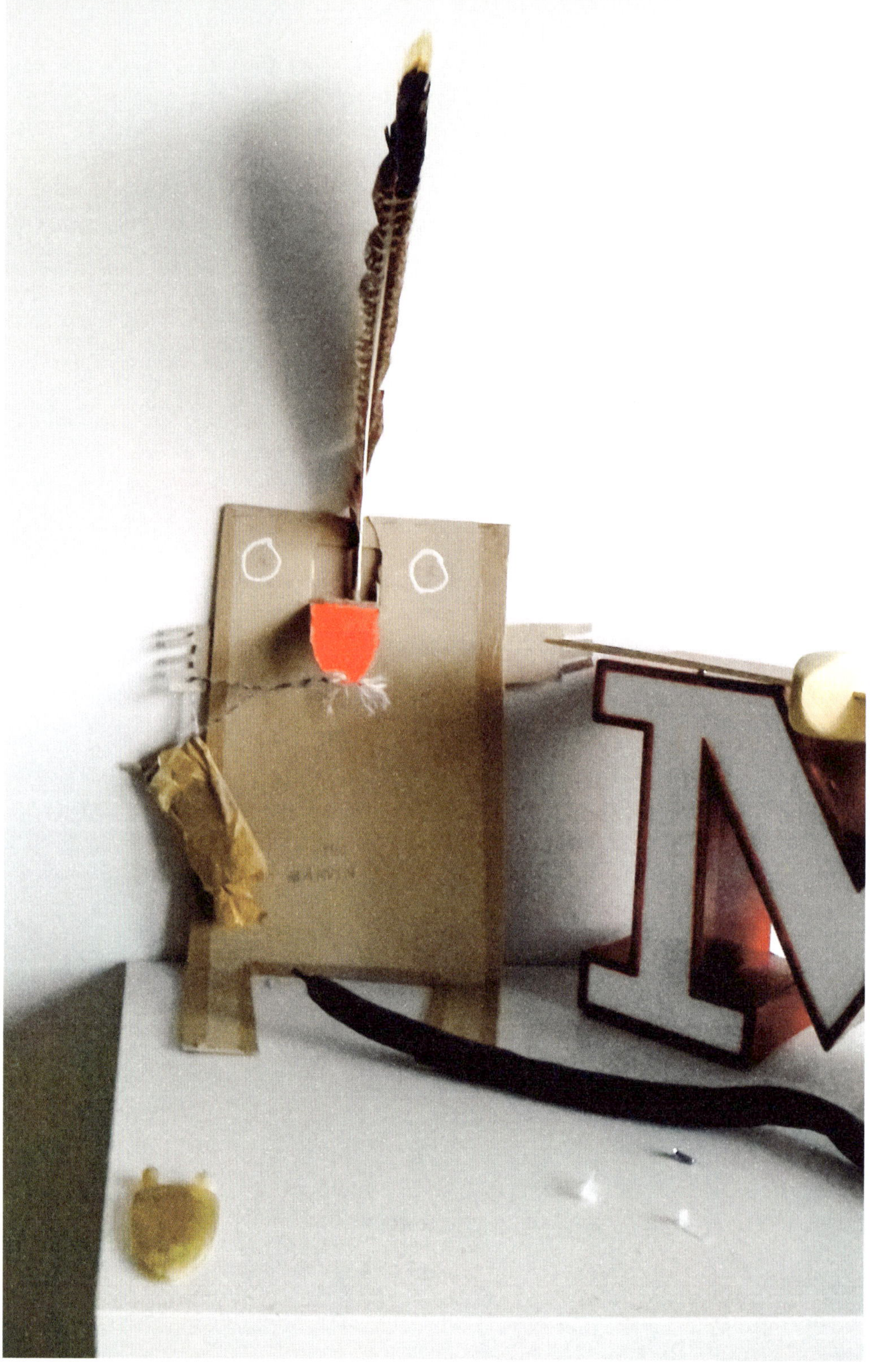

3 CHILDREN   The most obvious analogy to the private altars of adults are the collections children keep in cigar boxes, cookie tins or little cardboard boxes used as treasure chests.

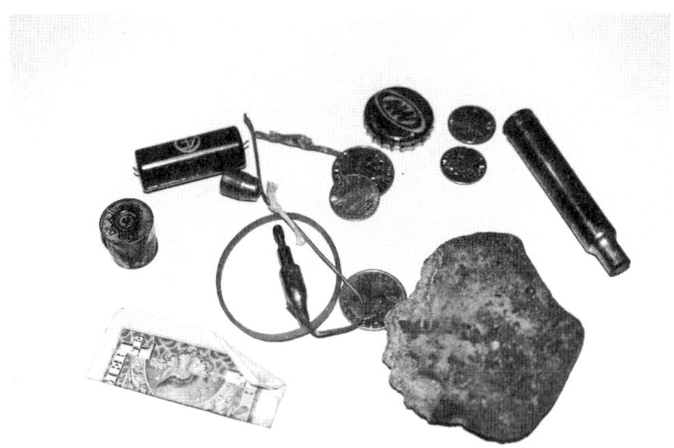

Tascheninhalt eines Knaben / The contents of a boy's pocket,
It's A Small Town Life! (Blog), 2009

Children's collections seldom include objects they actually play with; they mostly comprise found objects that are often removed from their original context: a fossilized shark's tooth, a Playmobil figure, two Pokémon cards, a crystal, a little cup with a picture of the Lorelei on it. ... They are distant evocations of the tradition of the cabinet of curiosities.

They don't contain valuable items (at least not valuable to grown-ups), but *"things that matter"* (Sherry Turkle), which, in their way and through transference to other, often fetishized, objects, retain their importance in adulthood. *"We find it familiar to consider objects as useful or aesthetic, as necessities or vain indulgences. We are on less familiar ground when we consider objects as companions to our emotional lives or as provocations to thought. The notion of evocative objects brings together this two less familiar ideas, underscoring the inseparability of thought and feeling in our relationship to things. We think with the objects we love; we love the objects we think with."*[9]

The things of private altars do not refer to some macrocosmic order; their arrangement forms a separate (self-refe-

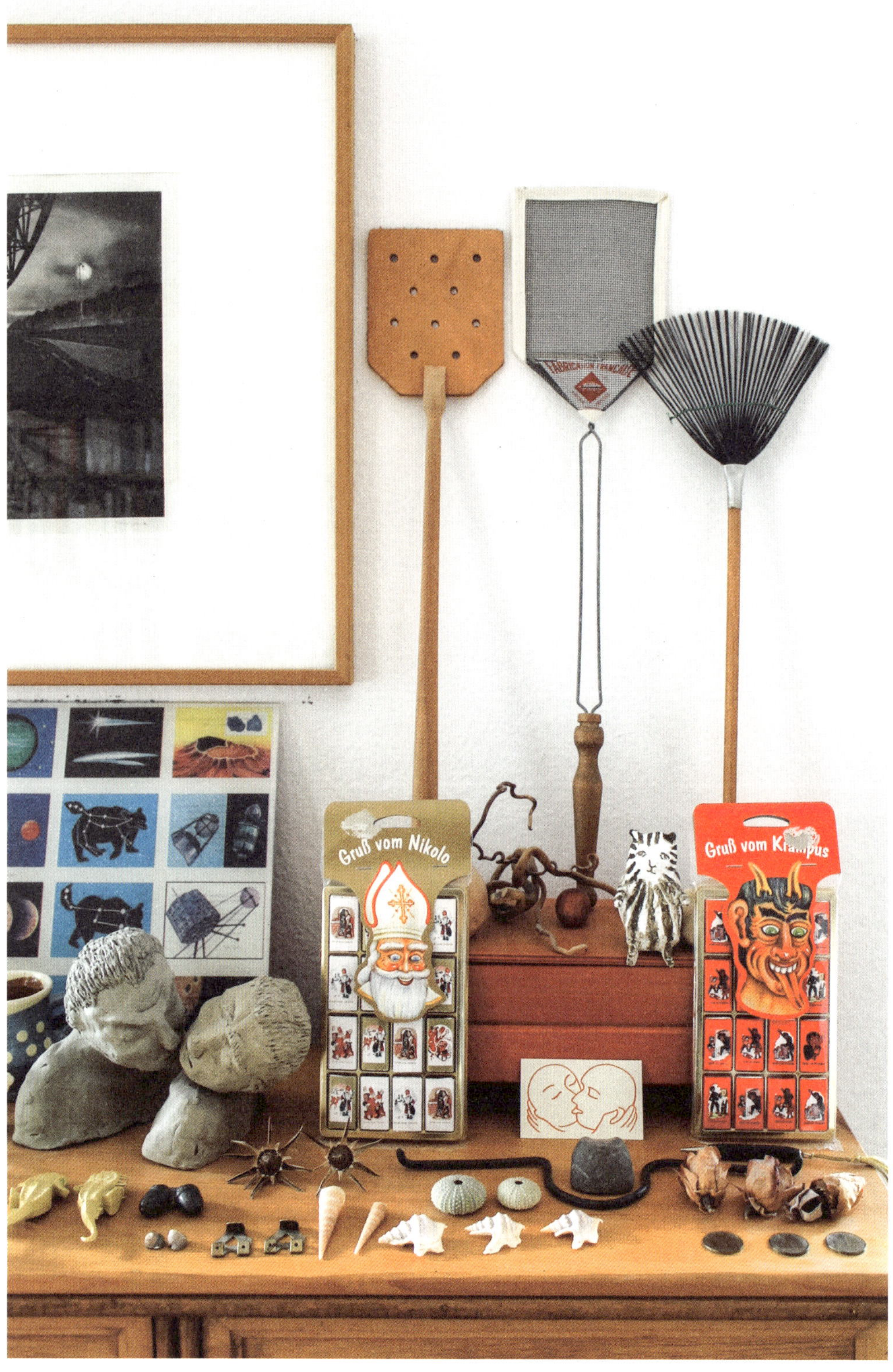
Gruß vom Nikolo
FABRICATION FRANÇAISE
Gruß vom Krampus

rential) microcosm instead. Like the secular family altars (to stick to this hallowed concept) of adults, neither the component items nor the whole of a child's collection can be chaincluded or, generally speaking, according to any discernible principle of collection. *"Children's treasures generally cannot be recognized as such and appreciated by adults,"* writes Burkhard Fuhs, which is precisely what affords children the opportunity to appropriate these treasures: *"In consumer society children have plenty of possessions, whose use, however, is regimented, and they have very little property with which they can really do as they please. [...] The less valuable a thing is to adults and the less a thing can be classified as an adult possession, the more readily children can appropriate it. So it is by and large ordinary, worthless things that become the actual property of children."*[10]

With their collected bits and bobs and odds and ends, children presumably aren't the only ones to elude the adult hierarchy of economic value. The items composing private altars often seem to belong to a category of personal value as well, which is why they can be bought cheap at a flea market, for example.

9 *Sherry Turkle (Ed.):* Evocative Objects: Things We Think With. *Cambridge, MA: MIT Press, 2007, p. 5.*
10 *Burkhard Fuhs: "Der Zauber der Dinge in der Kindheit" (our translation). In: Christina Schachtner (Ed.):* Kinder und Dinge. Dingwelten zwischen Kinderzimmer und FabLabs. *Bielefeld: transcript, 2014, pp. 80 & 81.*

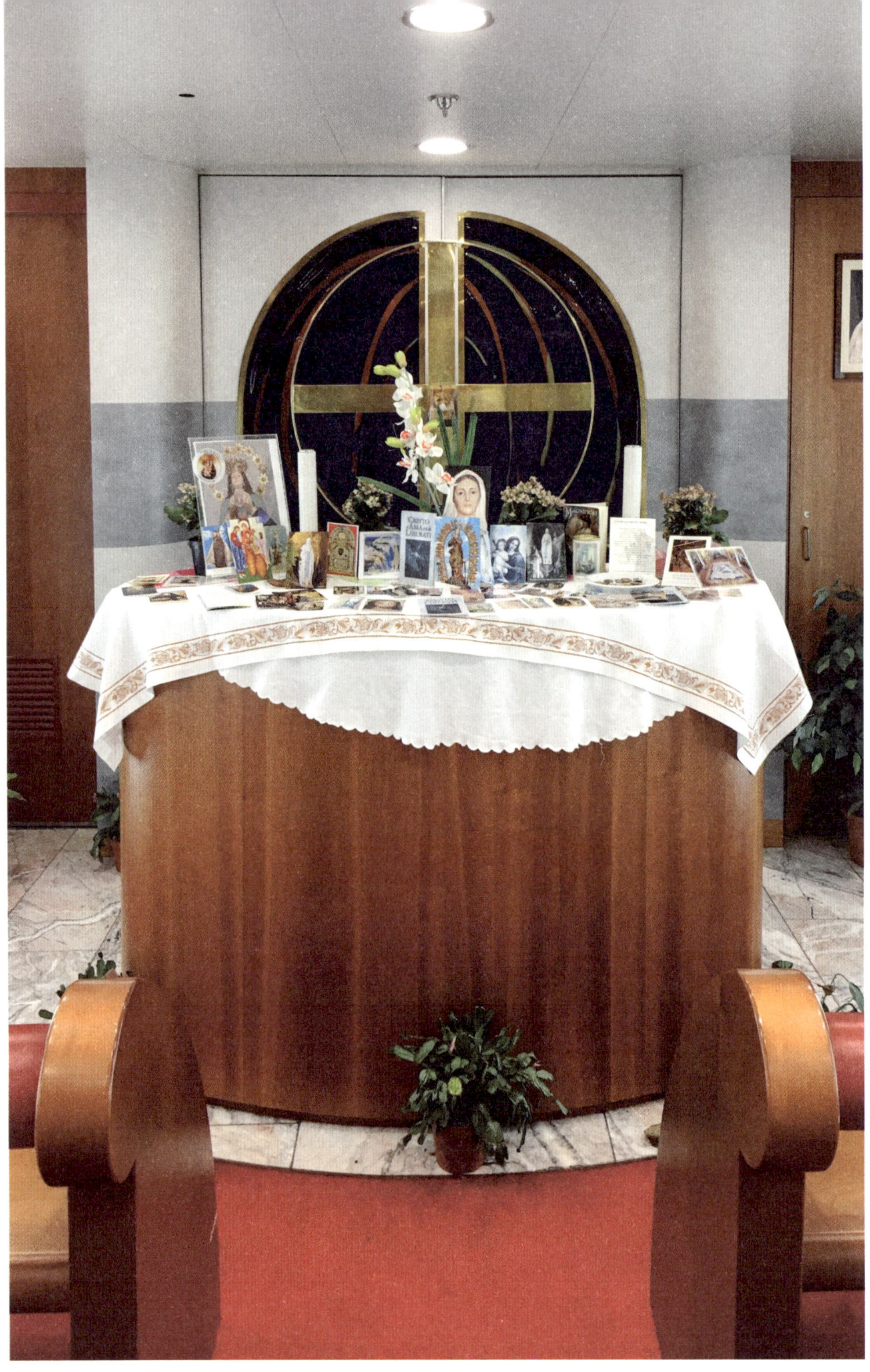

4 PATHOLOGY   The niche economy of children's collections, the private value hierarchy of private altars, has a pathological counterpart in what is vulgarly known in German since the 1980s as the *"Messie-Syndrom"* [sic].

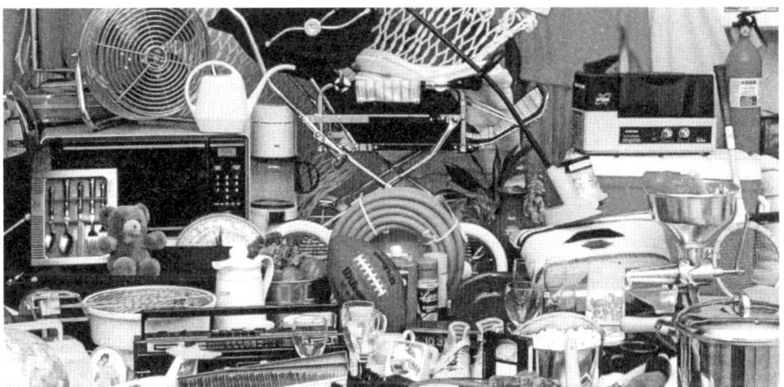

Flohmarkt / Flea market in Bangalore, *The Telegraph*, Indien / India, 2015

"Compulsive hoarding", as it is called in English, is first listed as a separate disorder in the fifth edition of the *DSM* (*Diagnostic and Statistical Manual of Mental Disorders* published by the American Psychiatric Association). Compulsive hoarding has since become a stock topic on TV shows that routinely treat the viewing audience to a peek inside the junk-strewn homes of their "messie" contemporaries.

A fancier term that has also caught on in German is *Wertbeimessungsstörung*: i.e. difficulty assigning value to things according to socially recognized standards.

But the creator of a private altar maintains an (ironic) detachment from the assembled objects, which a compulsive hoarder does not. One can, in theory, always add more items to private altars, but they don't tend to get mixed up with other household effects.

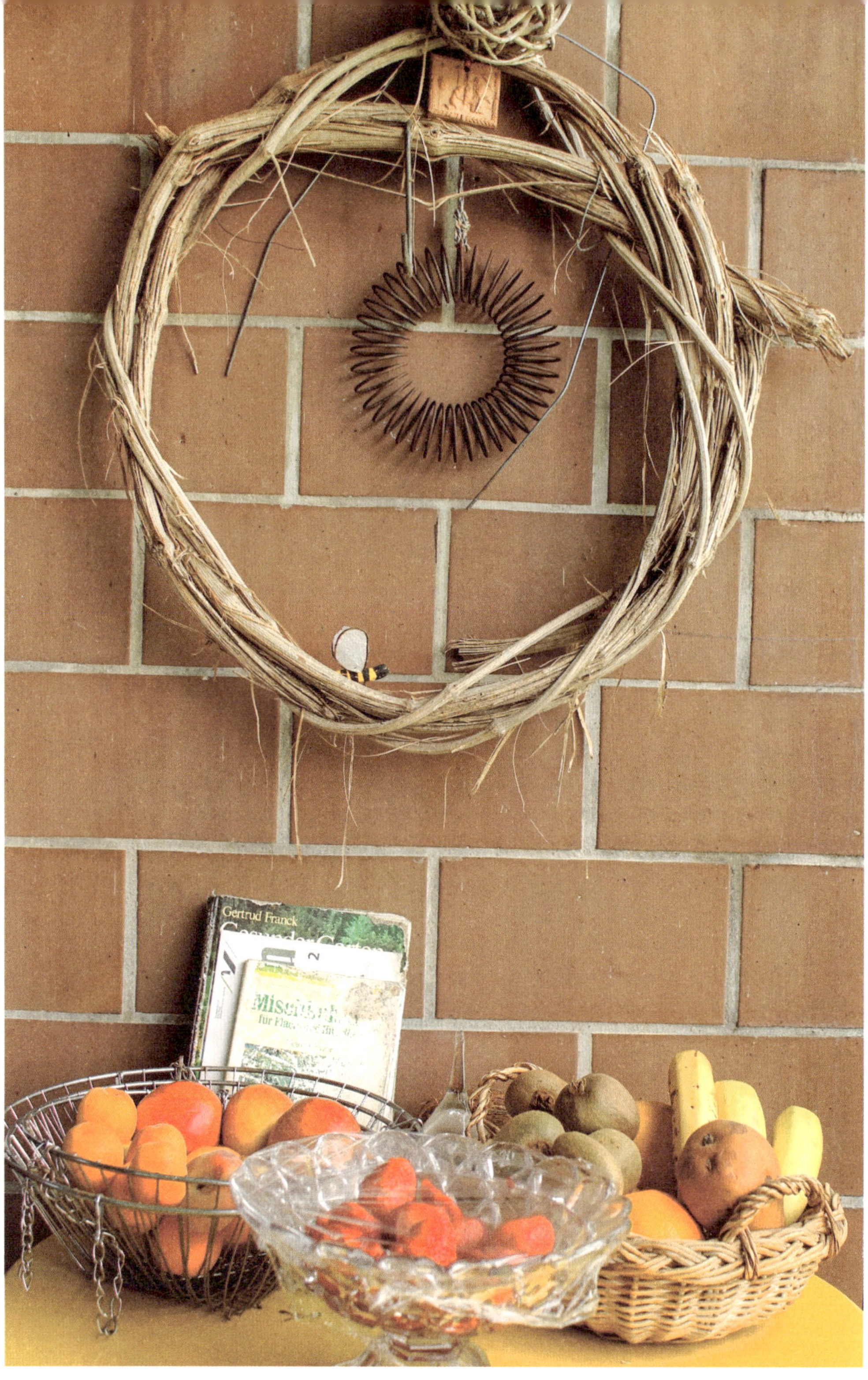

5 POETICS *The Comfort of Things* is a book by British anthropologist Daniel Miller, a field study of the residents of a street in south London.

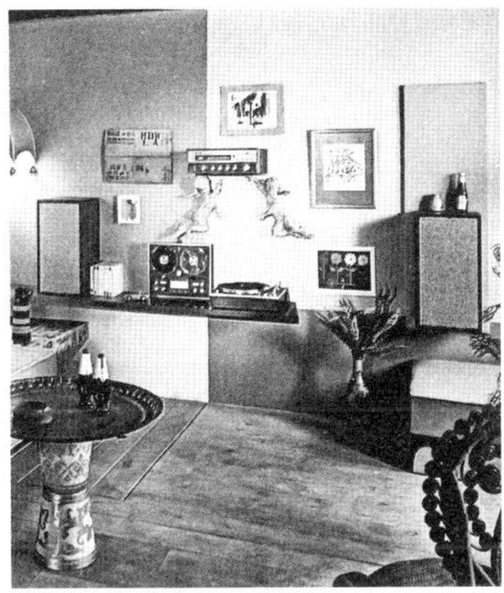

The Practical Encyclopedia of Good
Decorating and Home Improvement,
New York, NY: Greystone Press, 1970

"Objects sure don't talk. Or do they? The person in that living-room gives an account of themselves by responding to questions. But every object in that room is equally a form by which they have chosen to express themselves. They put up ornaments; they laid down carpets. They selected furnishing and got dressed that morning. Some things may be gifts or objects retained from the past, but they have decided to live with them, to place them in lines or higgledy-piggledy; they made the room minimalist or crammed to the gills. These things are not a random collection. They have been gradually accumulated as an expression of that person or household. Surely if we can learn to listen to these things we have access to an authentic other voice."[11]

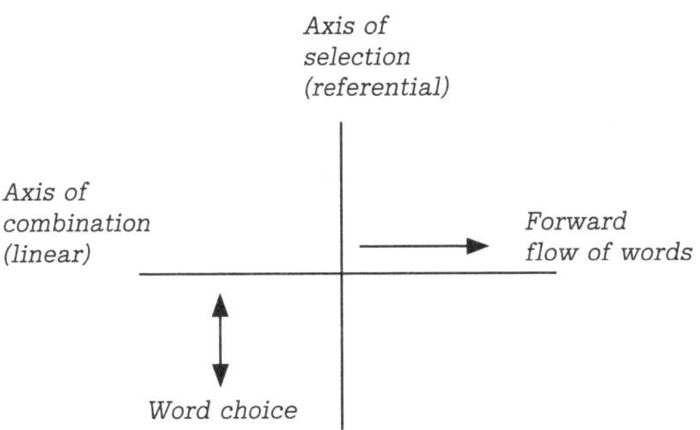

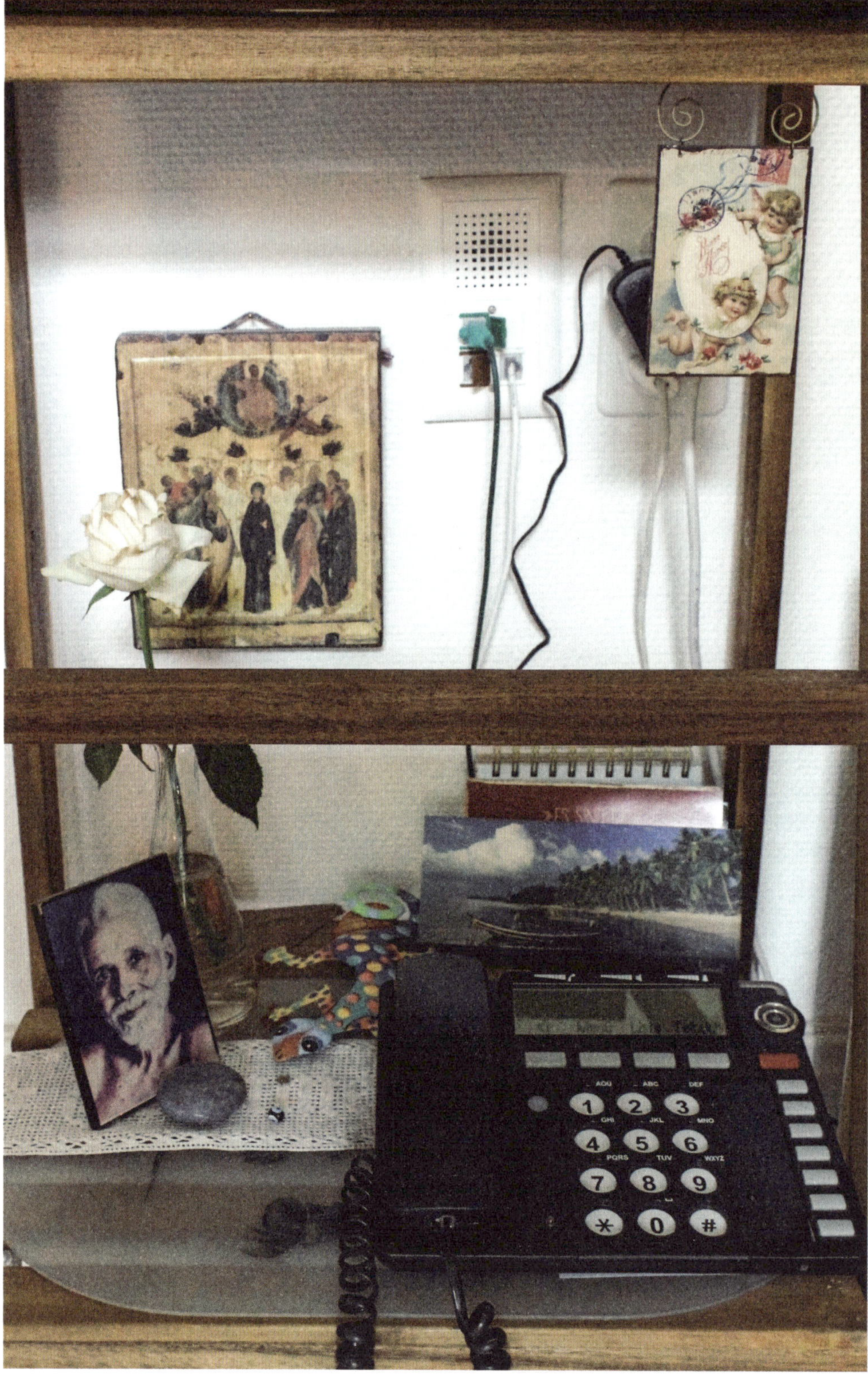

Whatever the things in a household may say to an anthropologist, they speak prose, as do their owners. They corroborate, round out or perhaps contradict what the householder says. The objects brought together on any private altar likewise partake of the murmur of things. But in a different register: they speak "poetically".

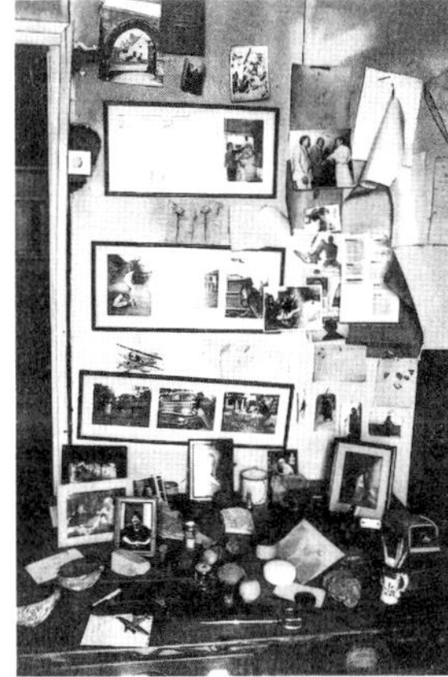

Roald Dahls Schreibstube /
Roald Dahl's writing shed,
New York Times Magazine, 2006

According to Roman Jacobson's classic definition of the poetic function of language, it *"projects the principle of equivalence from the axis of selection into the axis of combination. Equivalence is promoted to the constitutive device of the sequence."*[12]

What is combined sequentially in written or spoken language is combined by private altars in space, and according to a particular principle of equivalence that does not have a prior existence in language, but is established by that very combination.

This is why private altars seem a kind of enigmatic poetry within the casual prose of other things.

11 *Daniel Miller:* The Comfort of Things. *Cambridge, MA: Polity, 2008,* p. 2.

12 *Roman Jacobson: Selected Writings:* Poetry of grammar and grammar of poetry. *Volume 3 of Selected Writings, Roman Jakobson. Stephen Rudy (Ed.). Berlin: Walter de Gruyter, 1962, p. 27.*

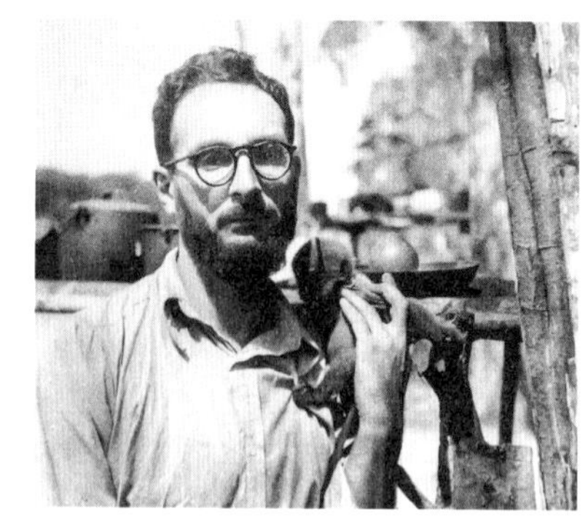

Claude Lévi-Strauss, Brasilien / Brazil, ca. / c. 1935

6 BRICOLAGE WITH LÉVI-STRAUSS *The "bricoleur" is adept at performing a large number of diverse tasks; but, unlike the engineer, he does not subordinate each of them to the availability of raw materials and tools conceived and procured for the purpose of the project. His universe of instruments is closed and the rules of his game are always to make do with "whatever is at hand", that is to say with a set of tools and materials which is always finite [...]. Consider him at work and excited by his project. His first practical step is retrospective. He has to turn back to an already existent set made up of tools and materials, to consider or reconsider what it contains and, finally and above all, to engage in a sort of dialogue with it and, before choosing between them, to index the possible answers which the whole set can offer to his problem. He interrogates all the heterogeneous objects of which his treasury is composed to discover what each of them could "signify" [...]. [T]he signified changes into the signifying and vice versa.*

This formula, which could serve as a definition of "bricolage", explains how an implicit inventory or conception of the total means available must be made in the case of mythical thought also, so that a result can be defined which will always be a compromise between the structure of the instrumental set and that of the project. Once it materializes the project will therefore inevitably be at a remove from the initial aim (which was moreover a mere sketch), a phenomenon which the surrealists have felicitously called "objective hazard".

Further, the "bricoleur" also, and indeed principally, derives his poetry from the fact that he does not confine himself to accomplishment and execution: he "speaks" not only with things, as we have already seen, but also through the medium of things: giving an account of his personality and life by the choices he makes between the limited possibilities. The "bricoleur" may not ever complete his purpose but he always puts something of himself into it. [13]

13 *Claude Lévi-Strauss:* The Savage Mind. *Translated by George Weidenfield and Nicholson Ltd., Chicago: University of Chicago Press, 1966, pp. 17, 18, 21.*

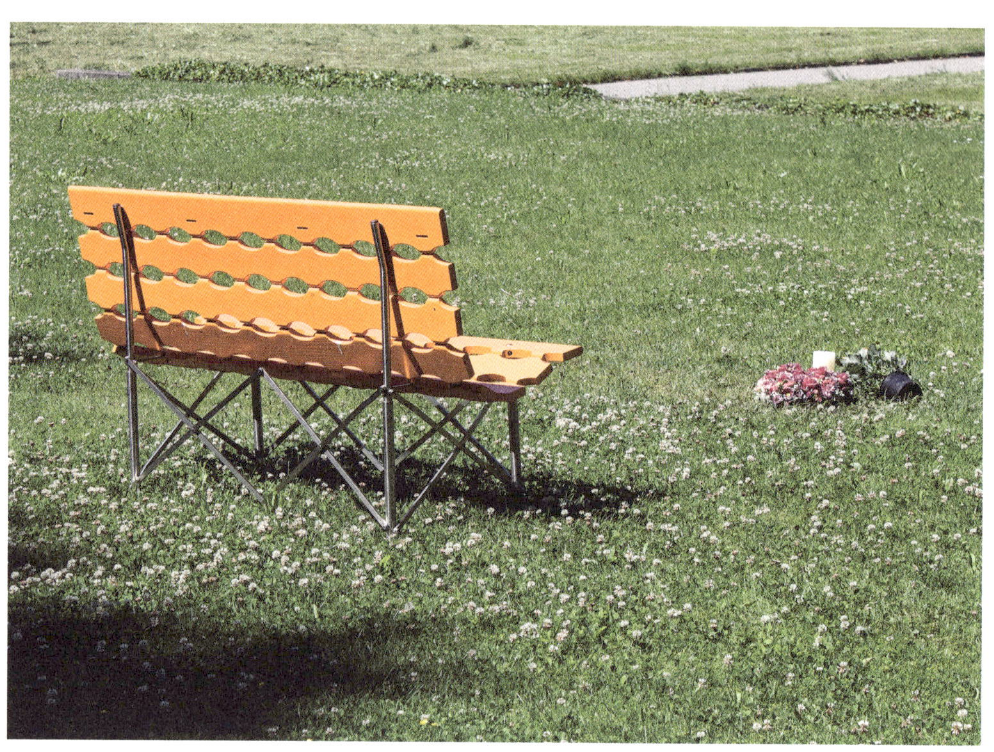

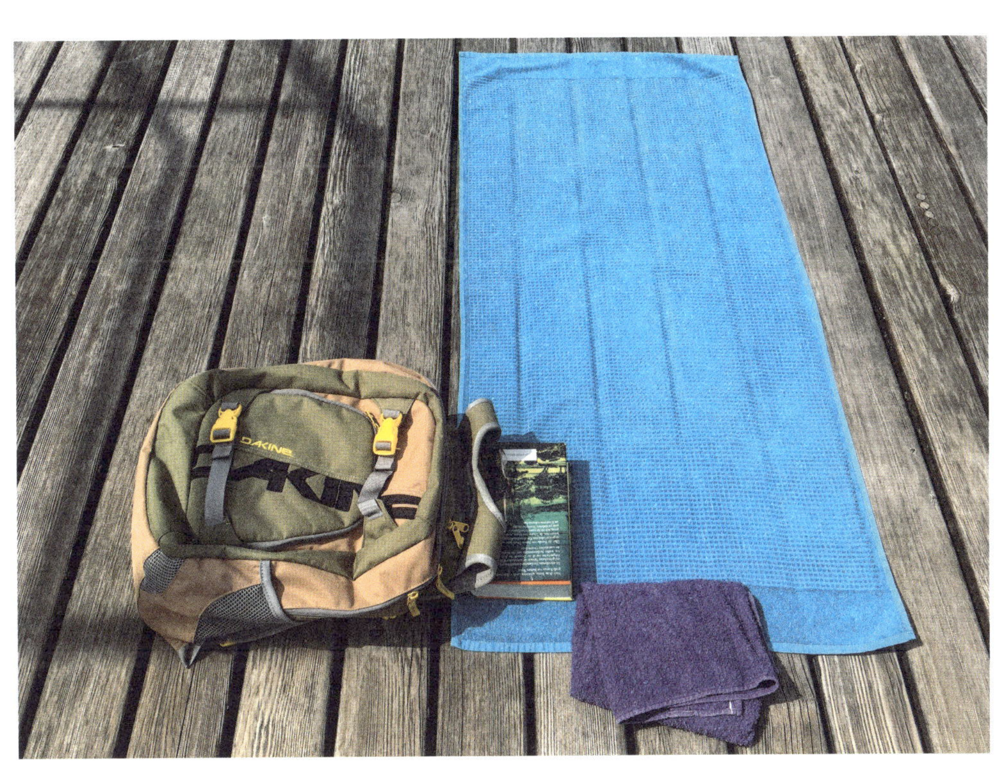

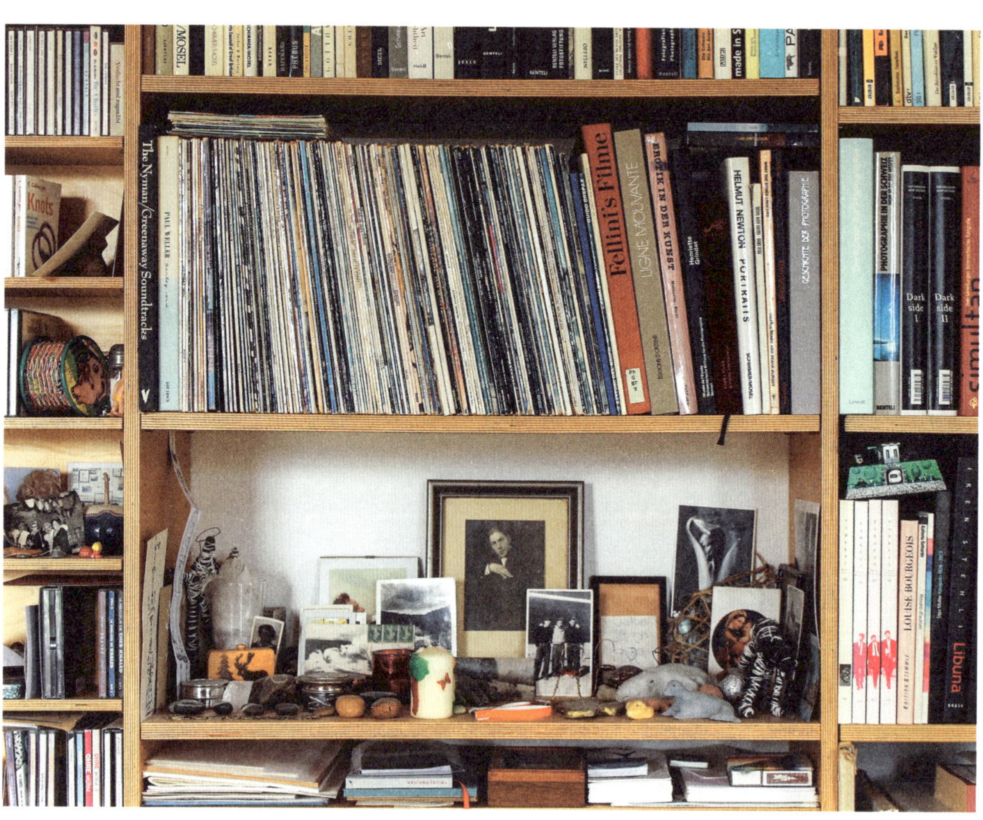

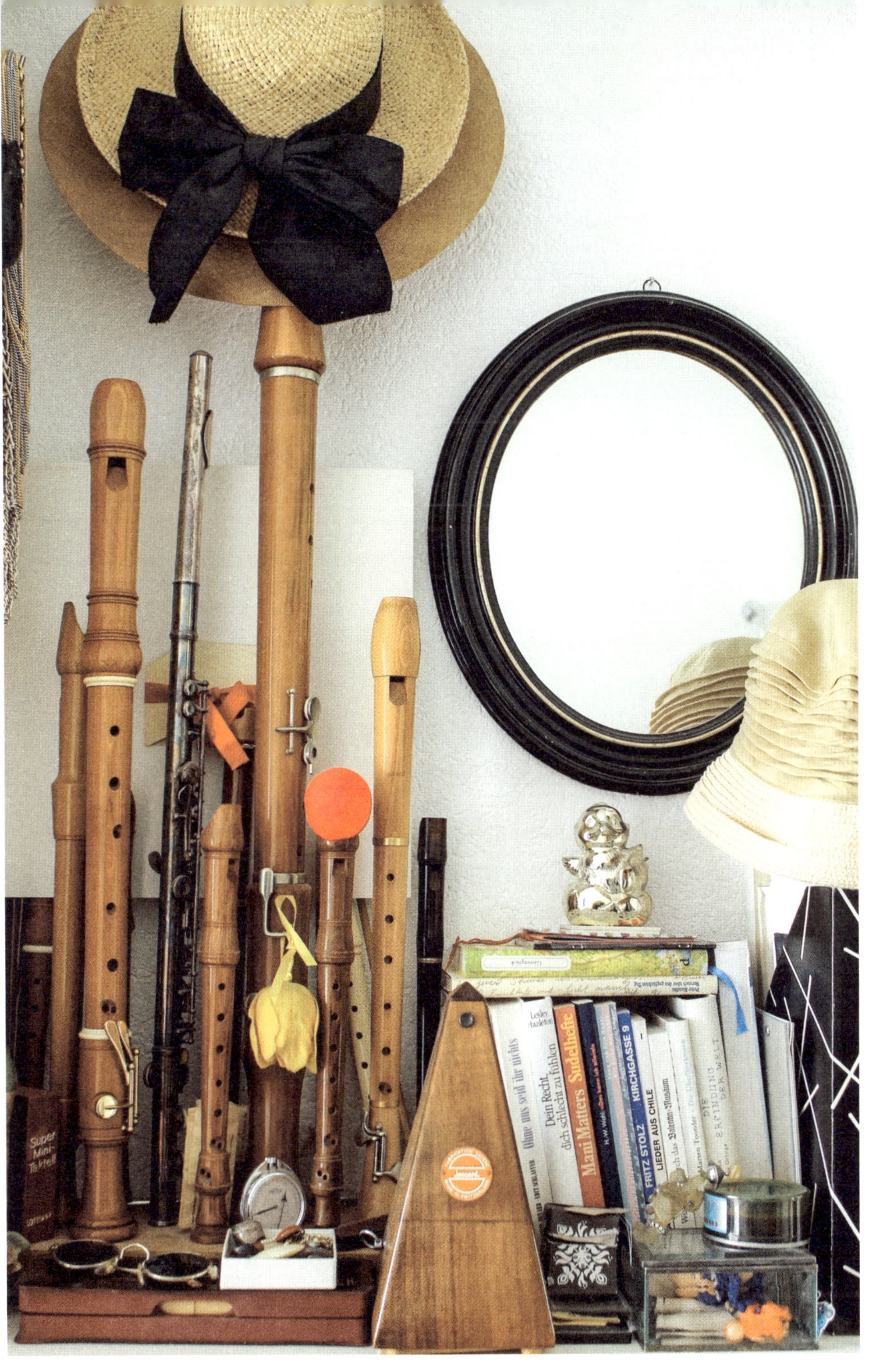

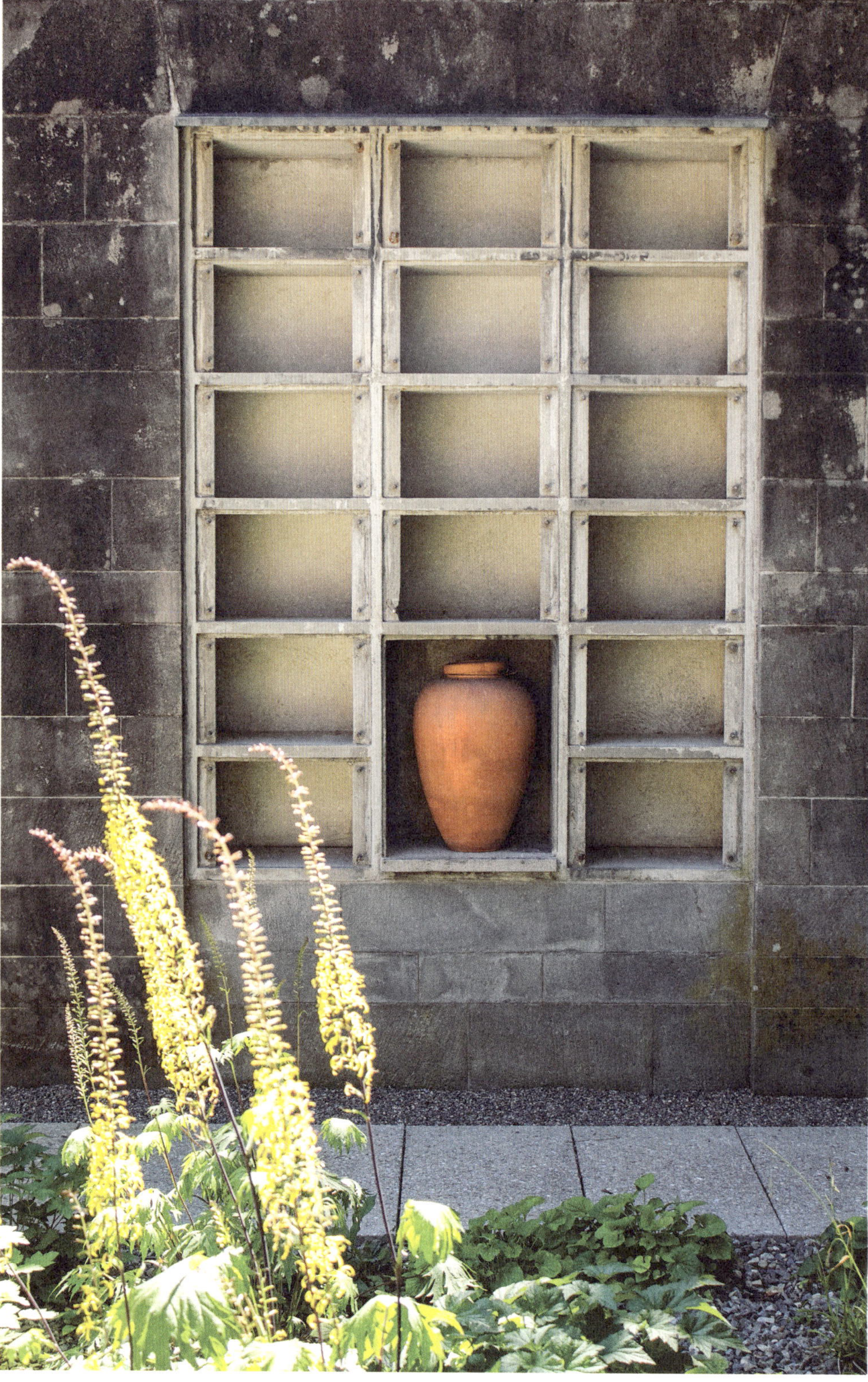

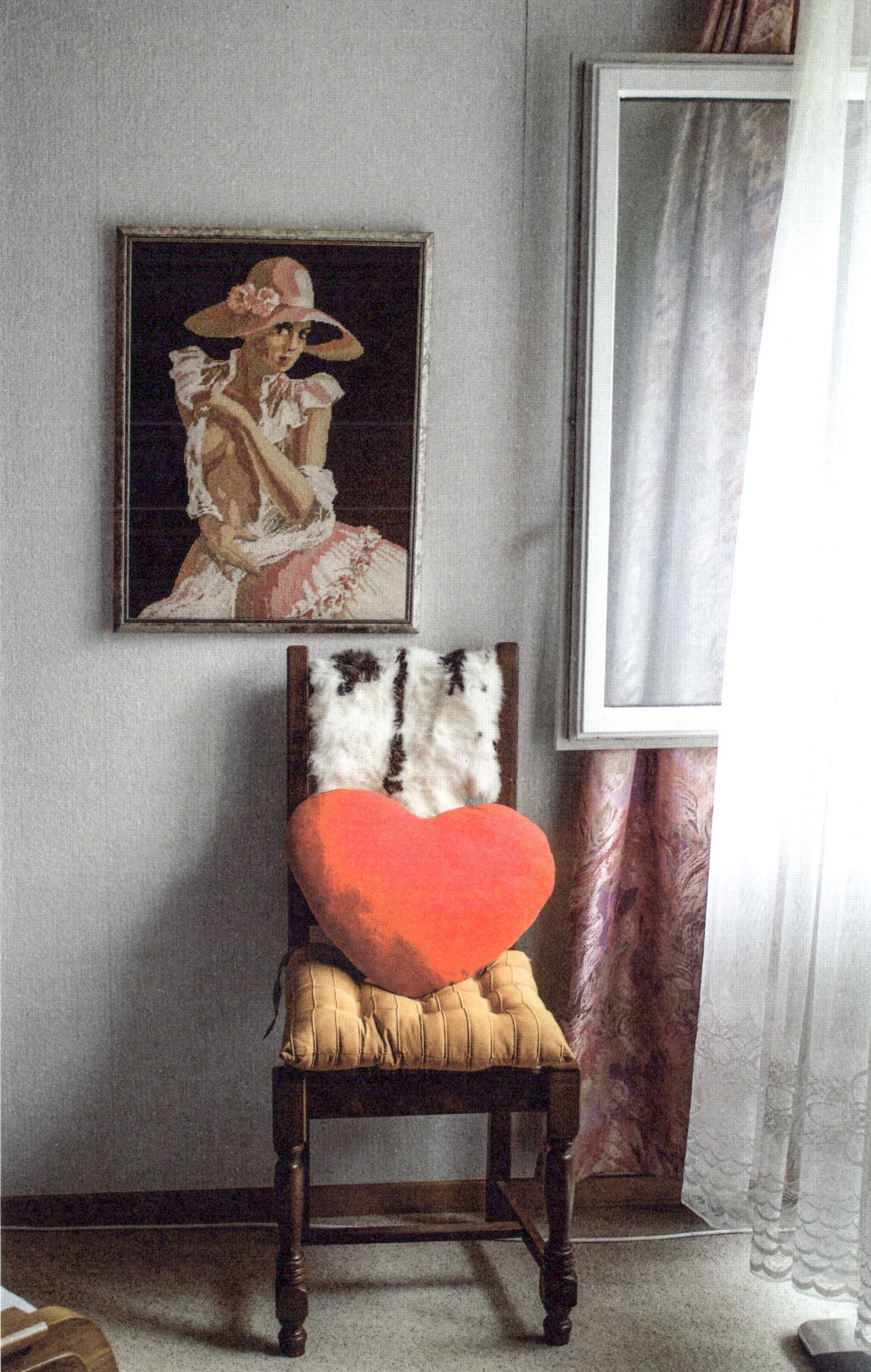

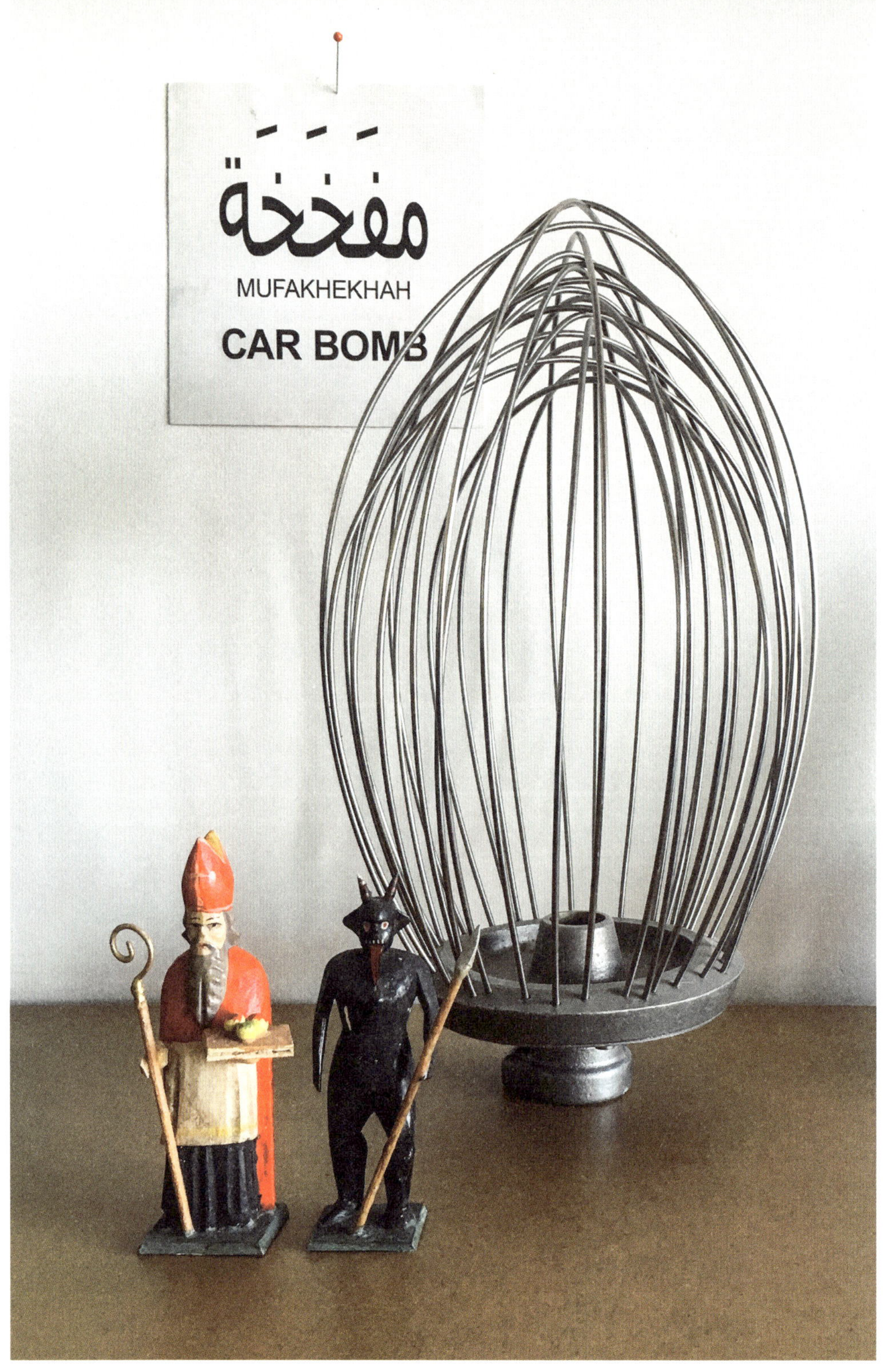
مفخخة
MUFAKHEKHAH
CAR BOMB

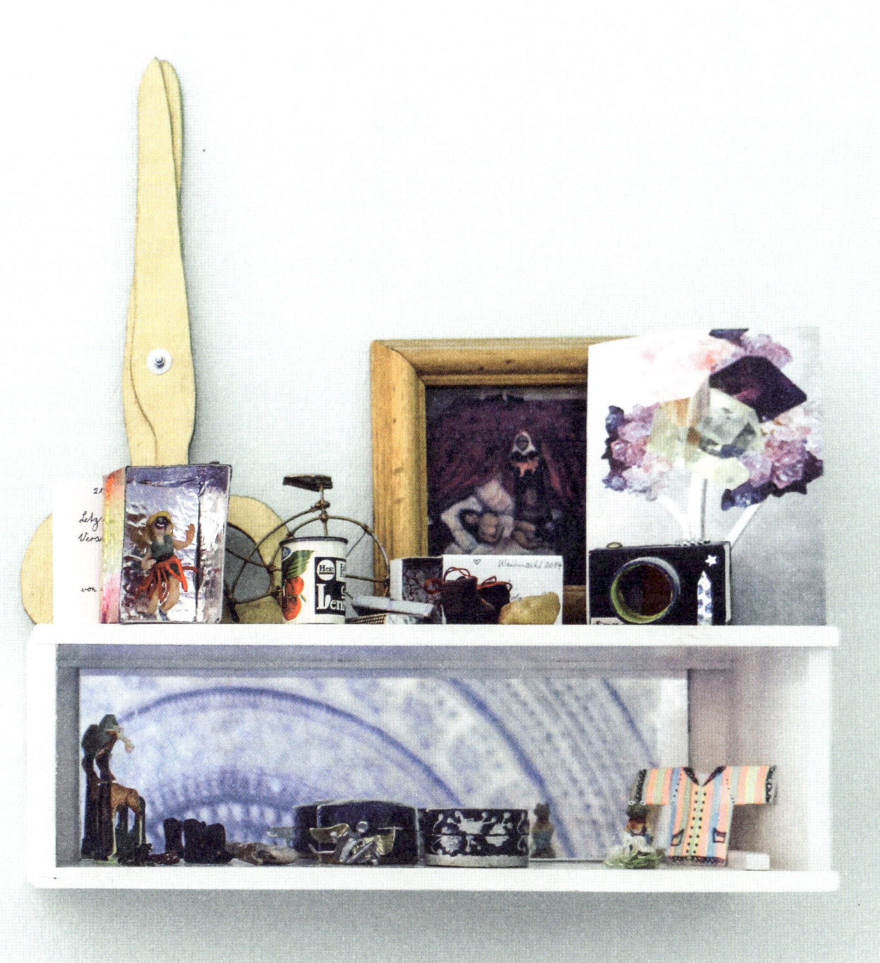

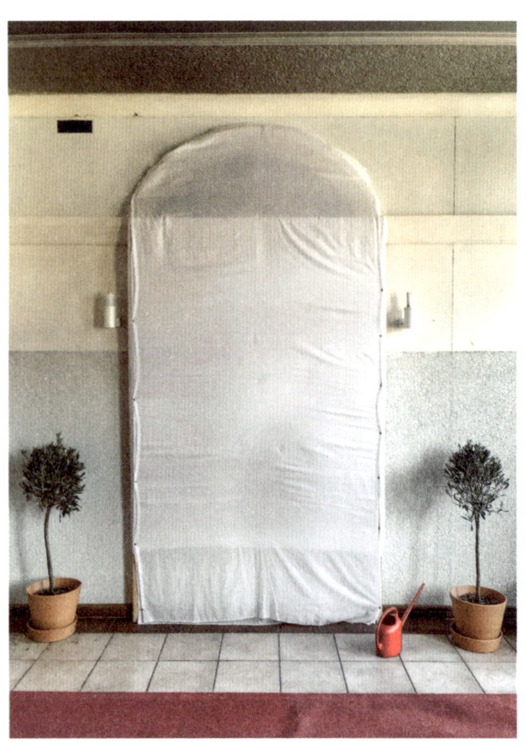

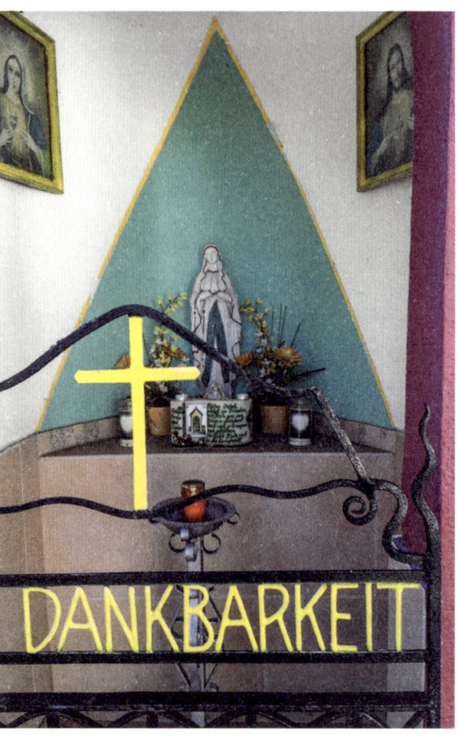
DANKBARKEIT

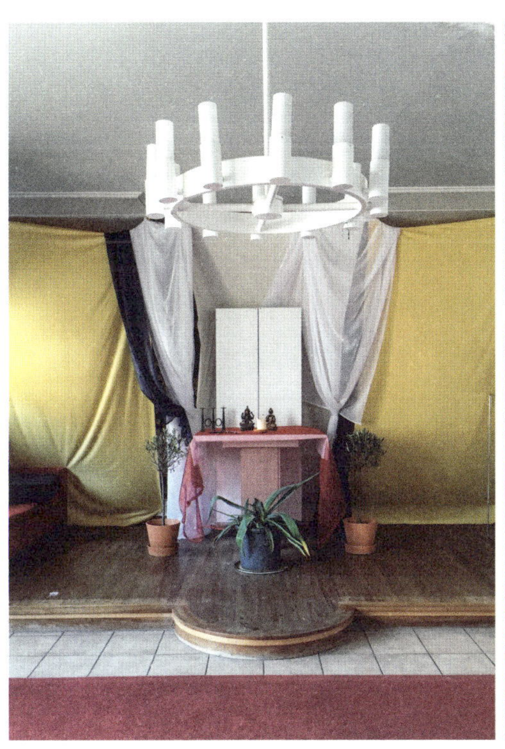 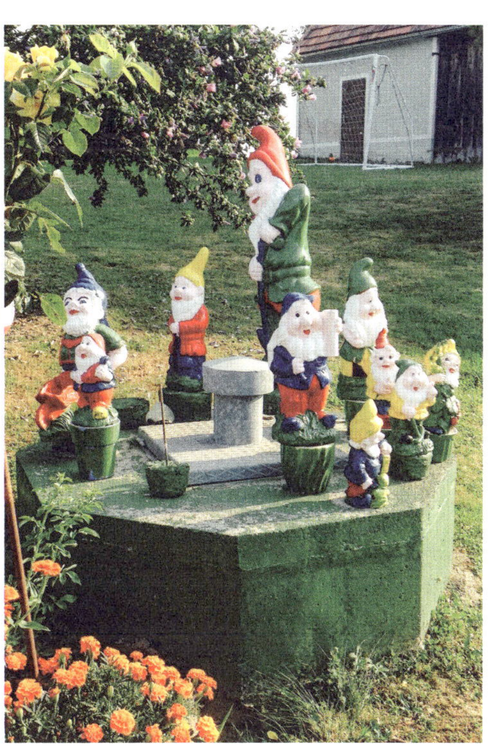

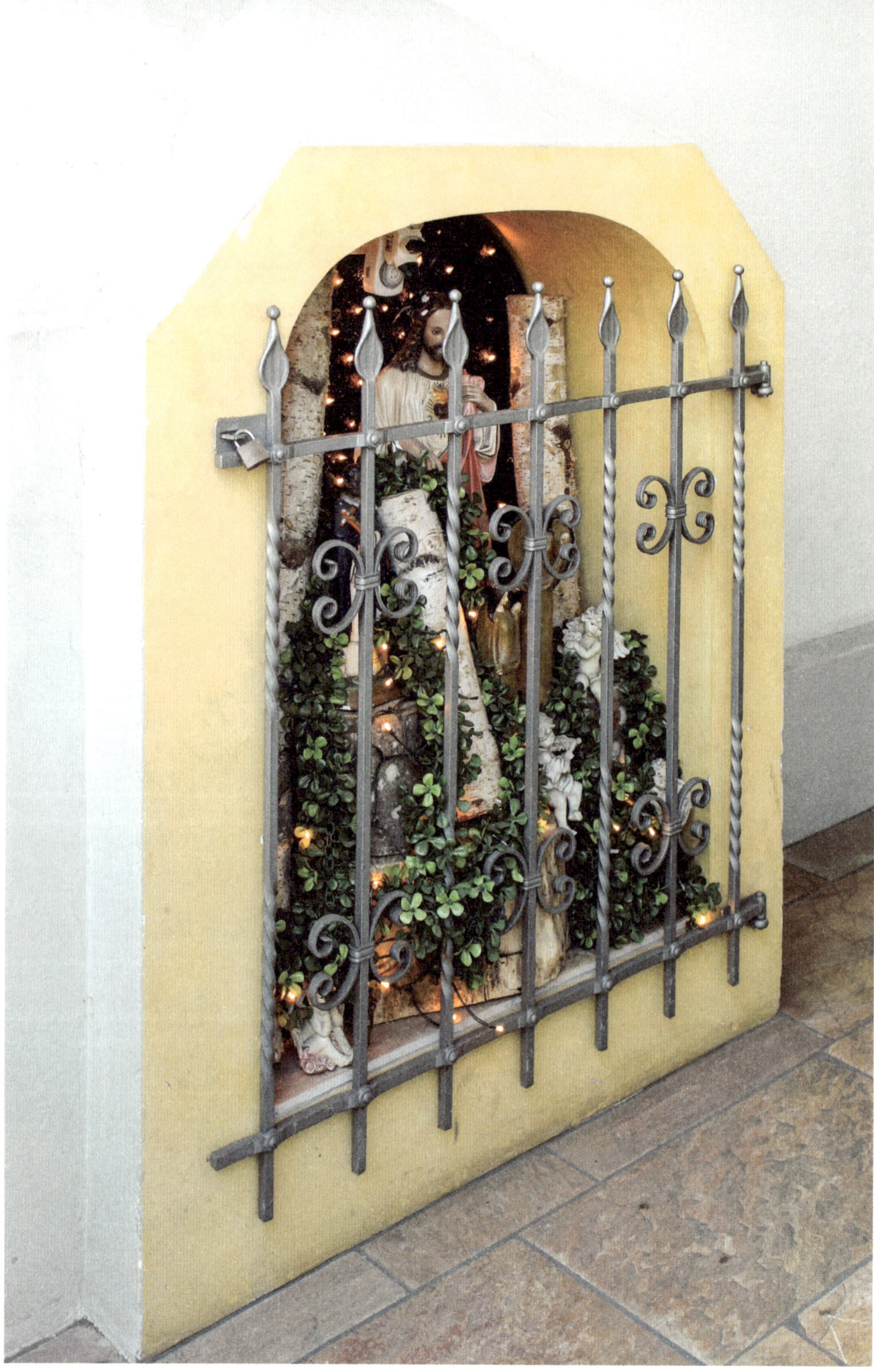

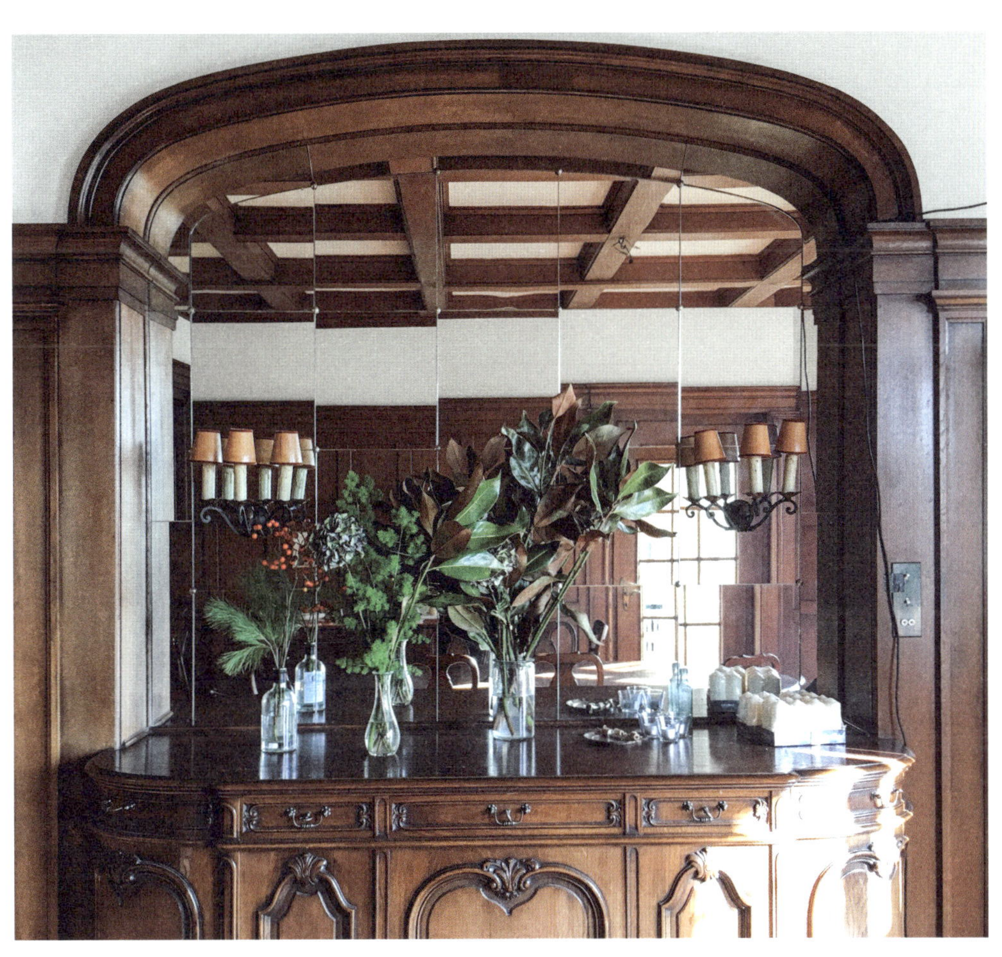

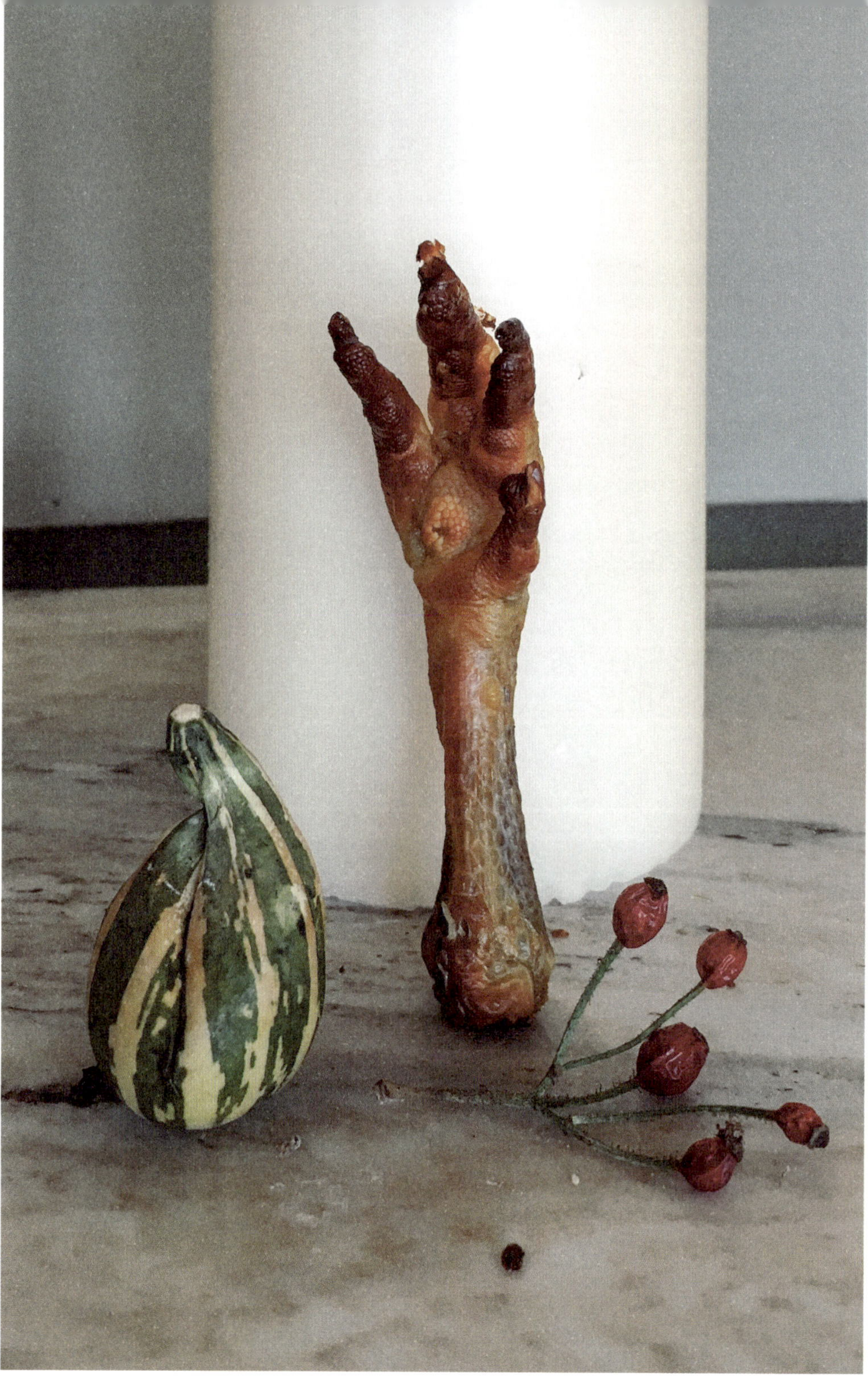

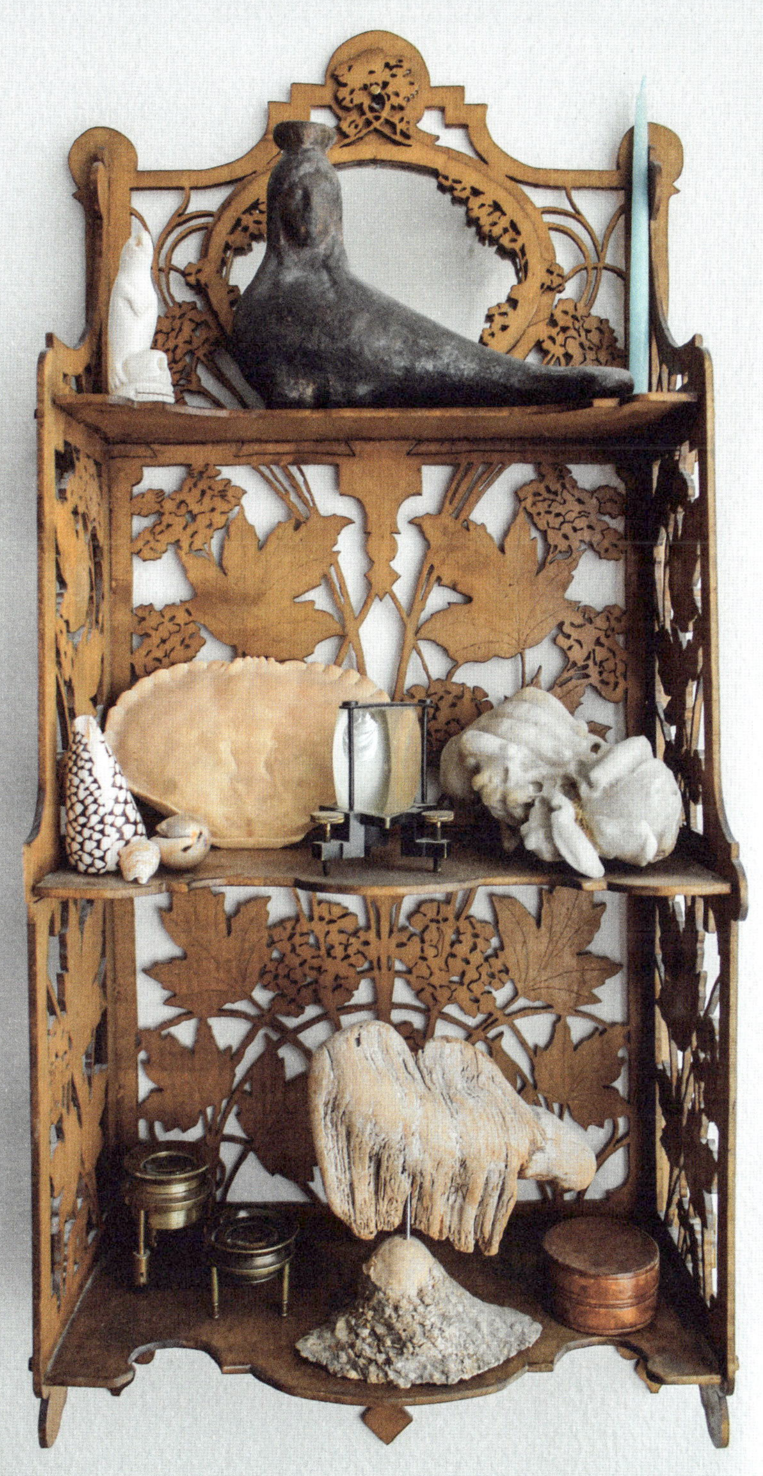

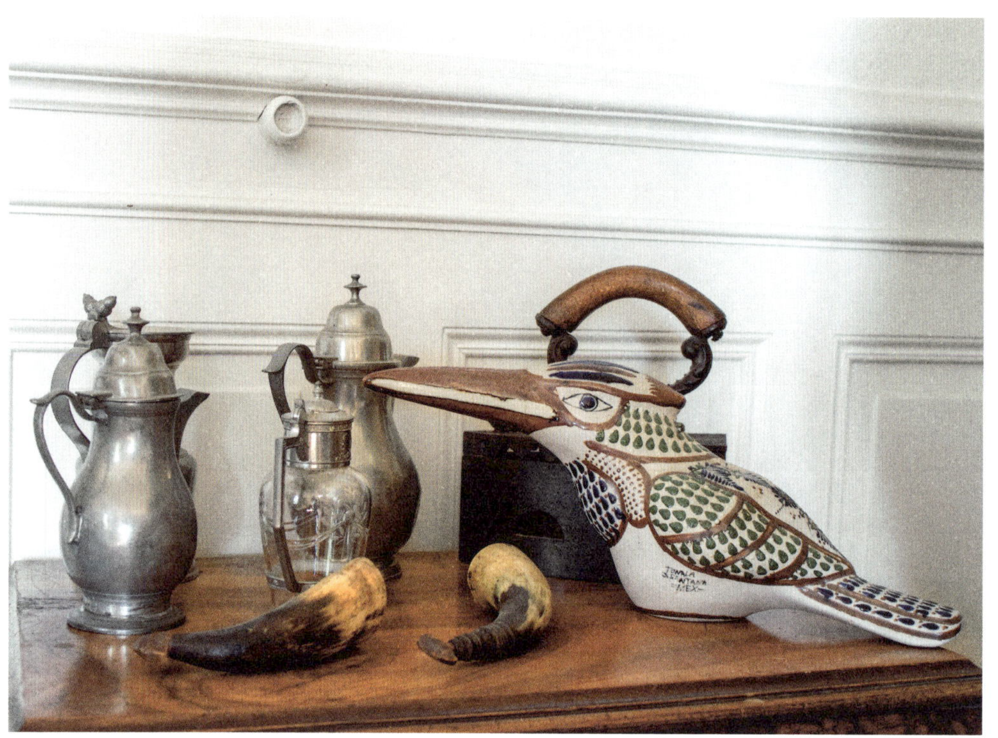

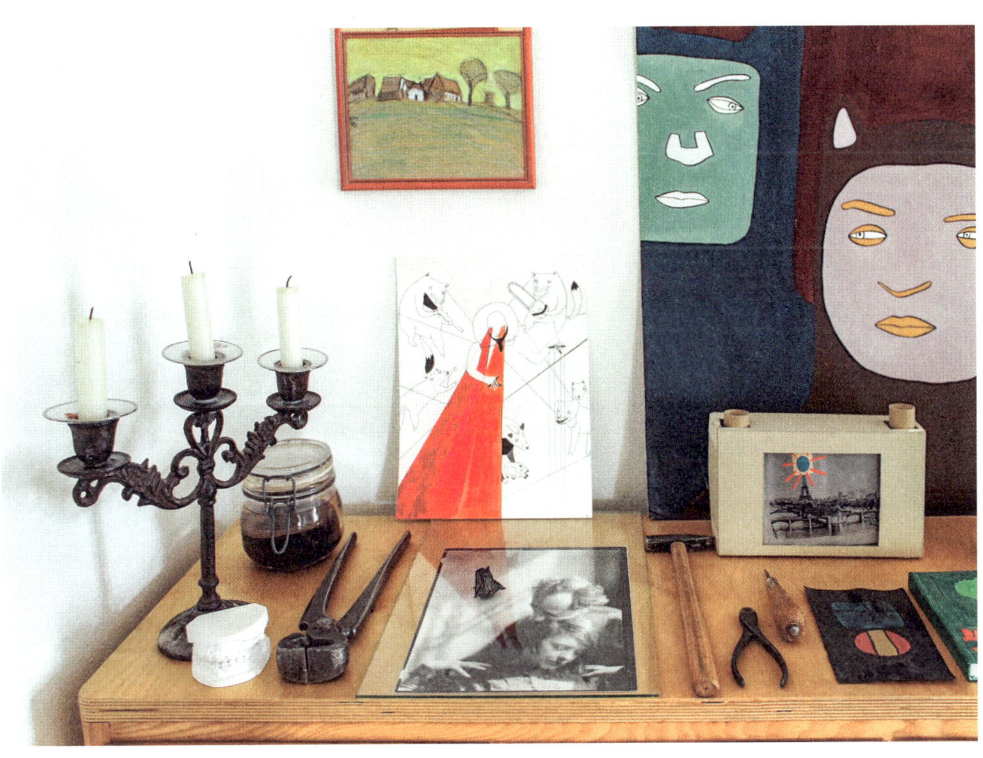

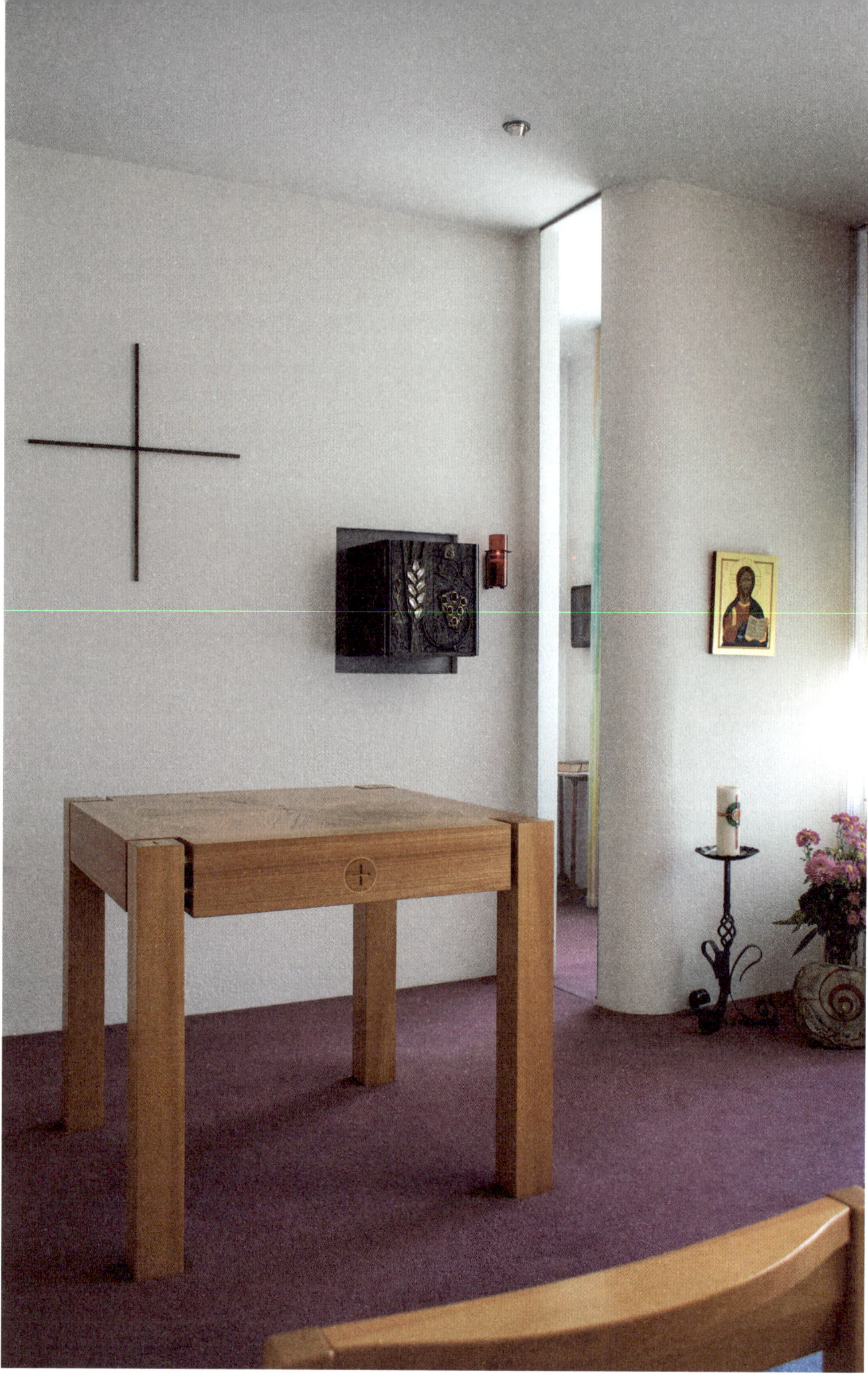

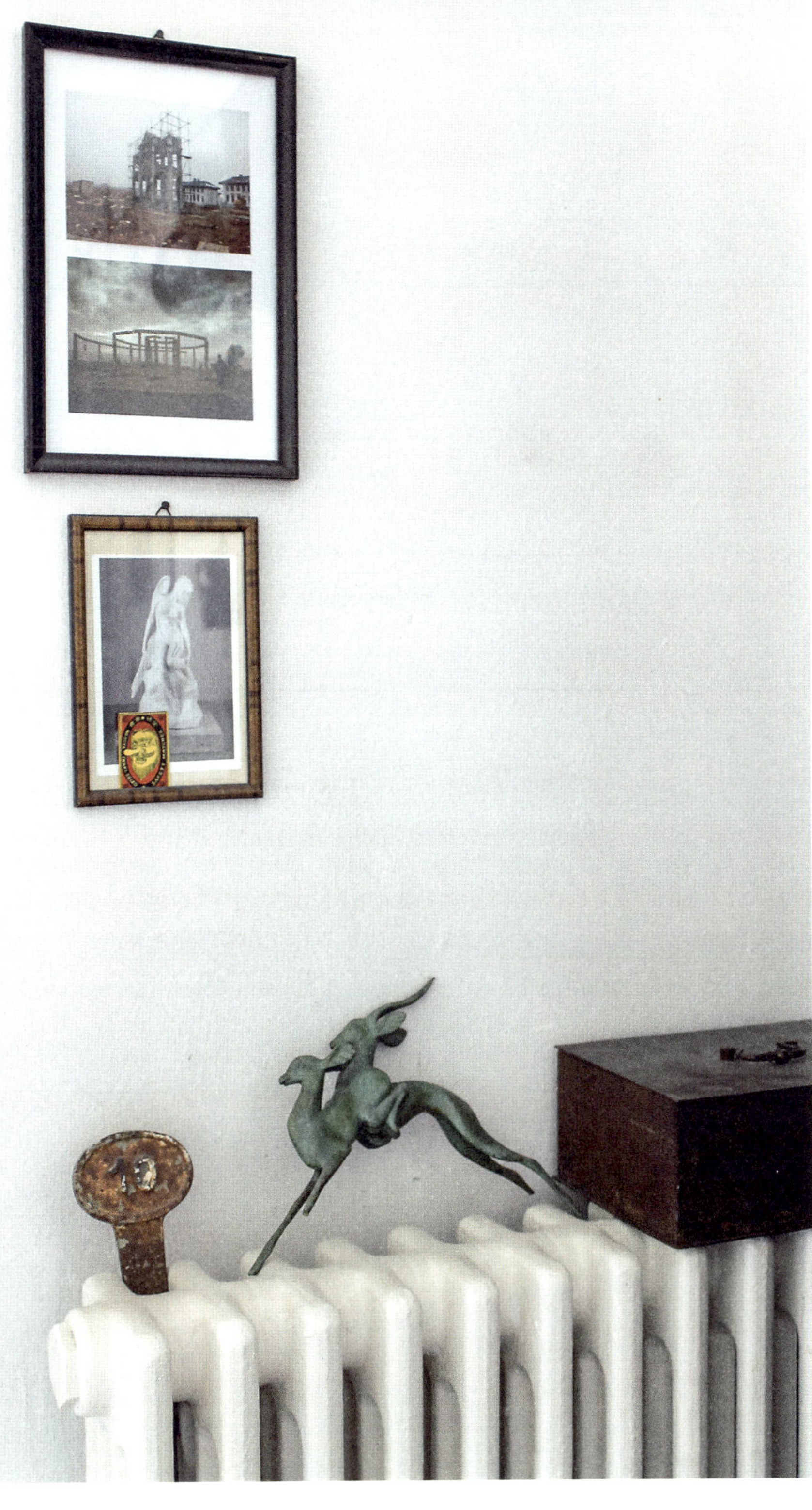

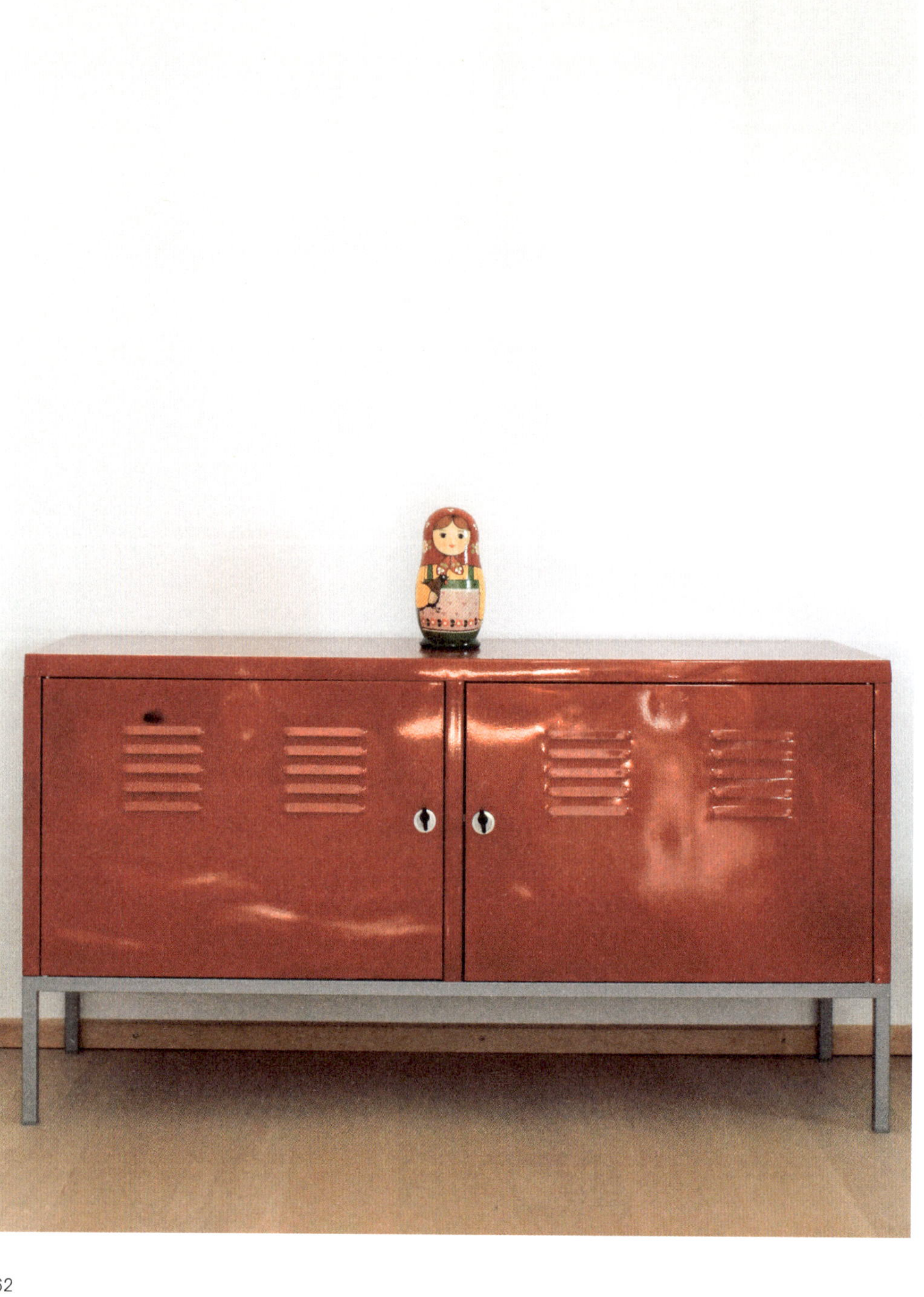

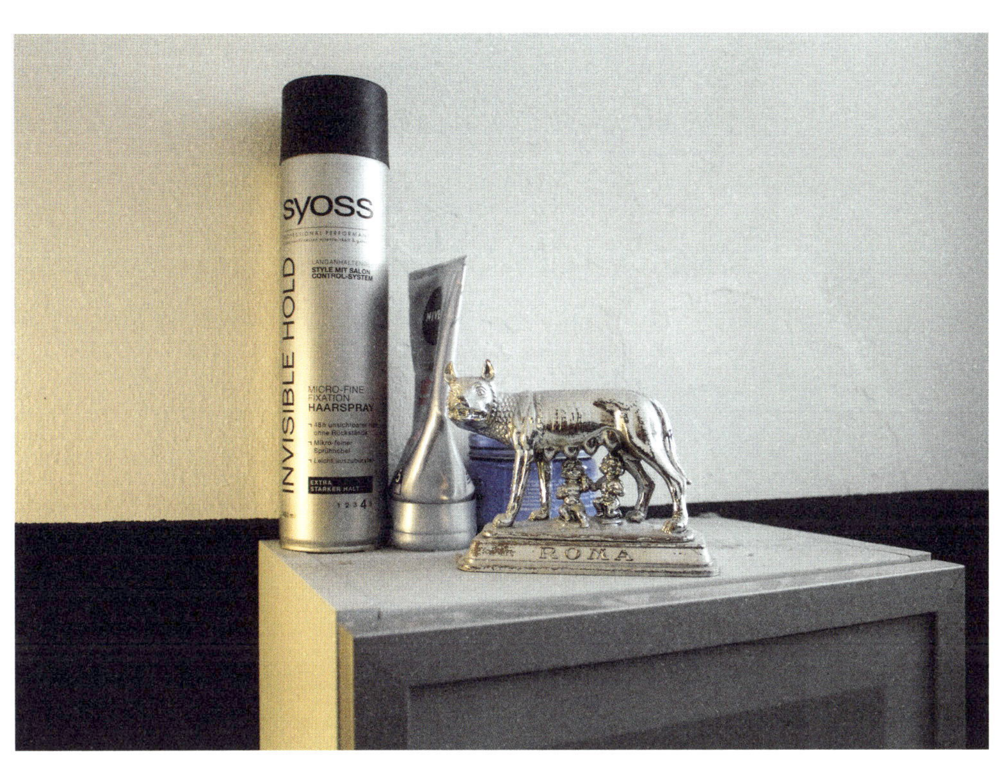
syoss
STYLE MIT SALON
CONTROL-SYSTEM
INVISIBLE HOLD
MICRO-FINE
FIXATION
HAARSPRAY
EXTRA
STARKER HALT
ROMA

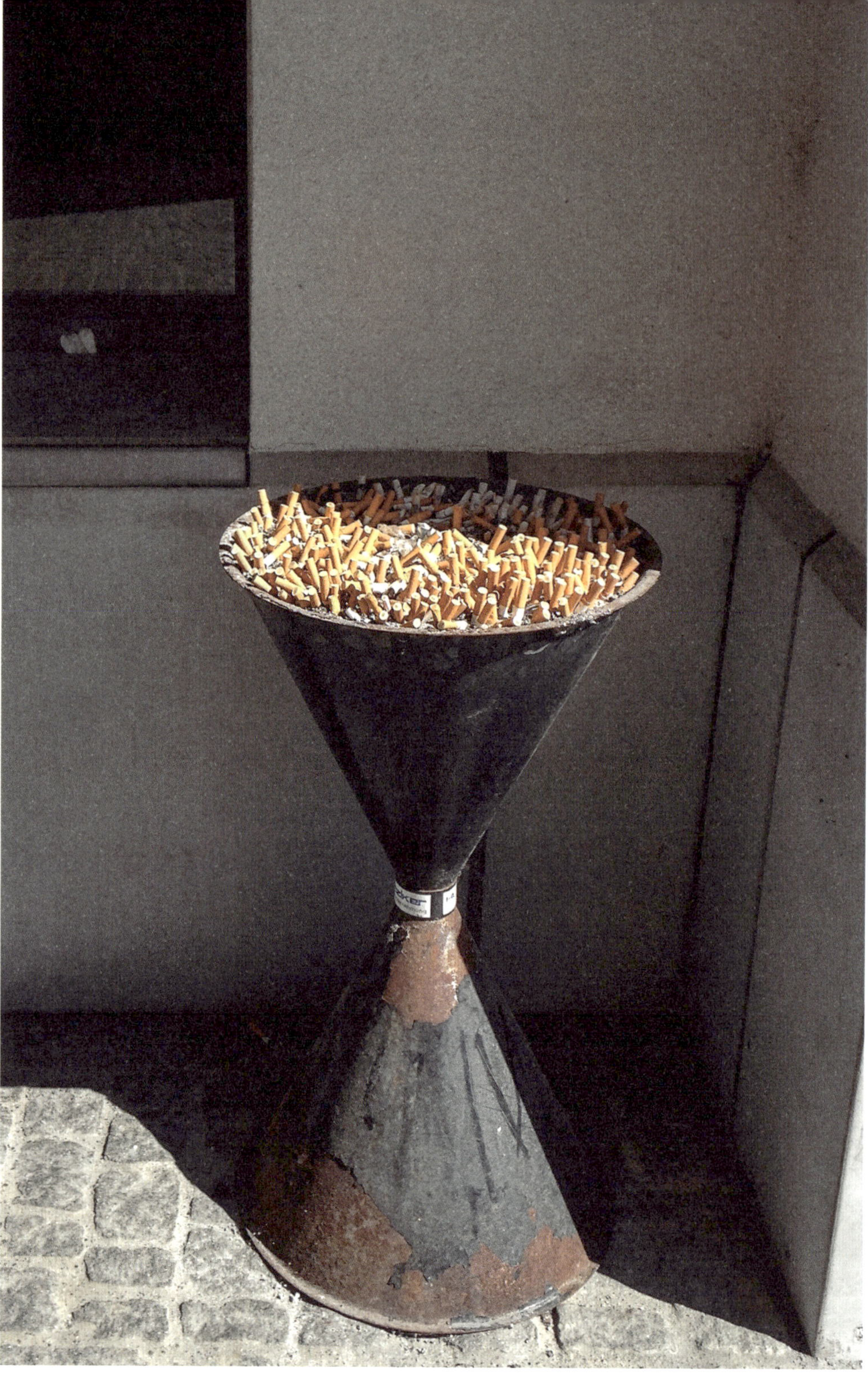

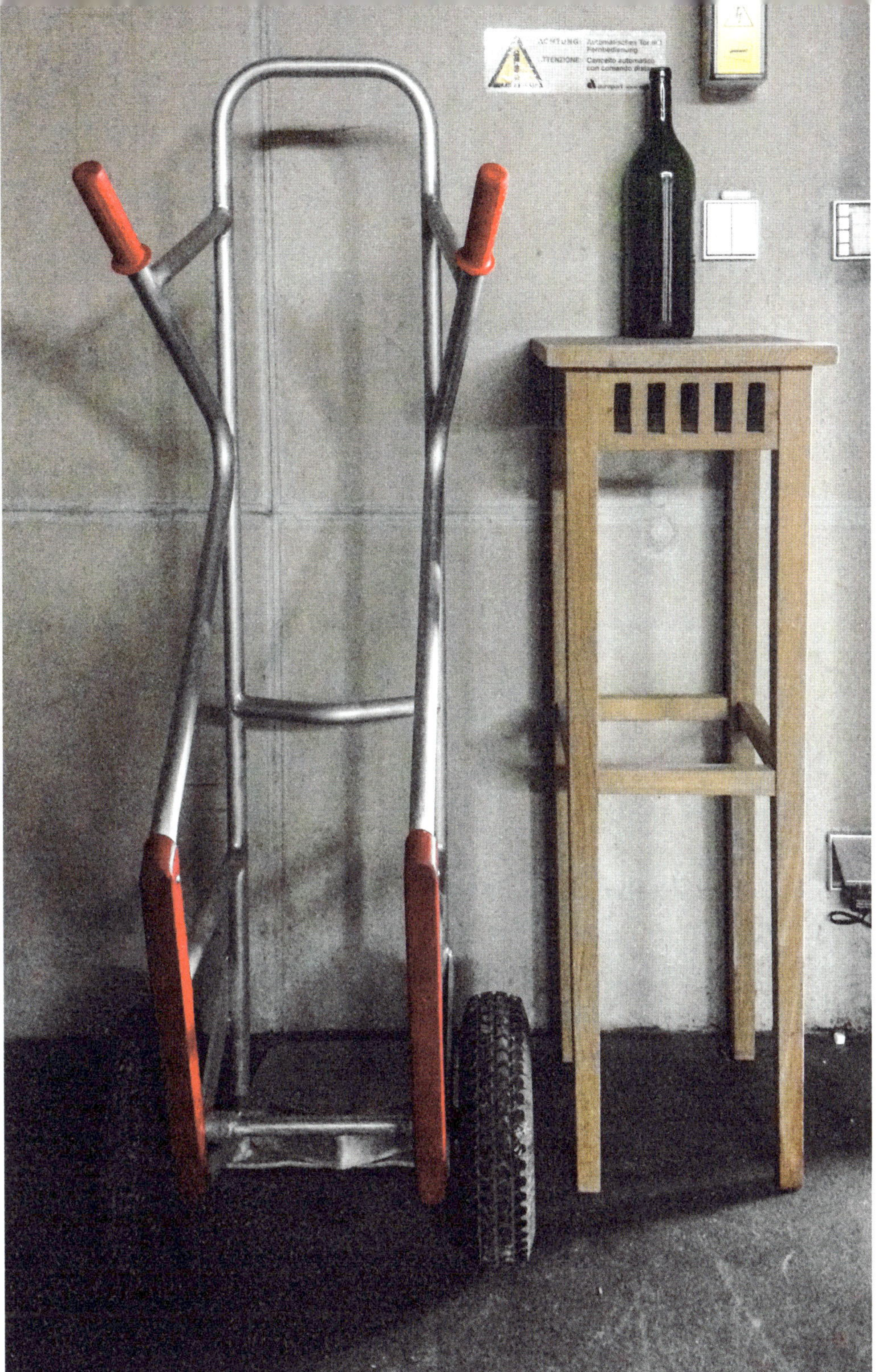

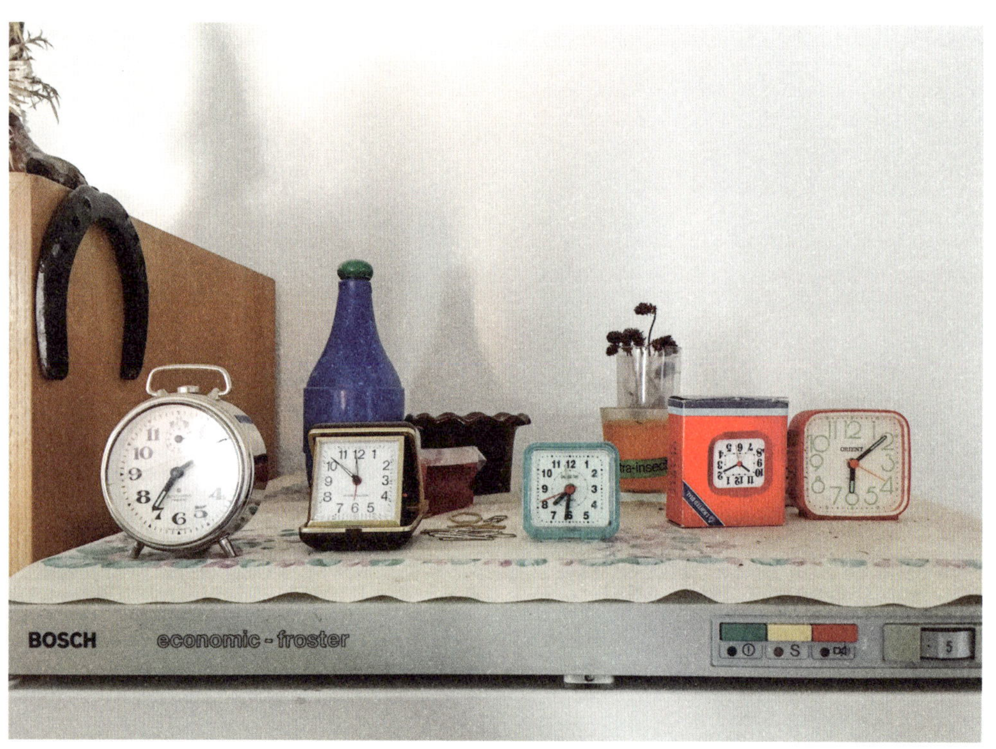

BOSCH economic - froster
ORIENT

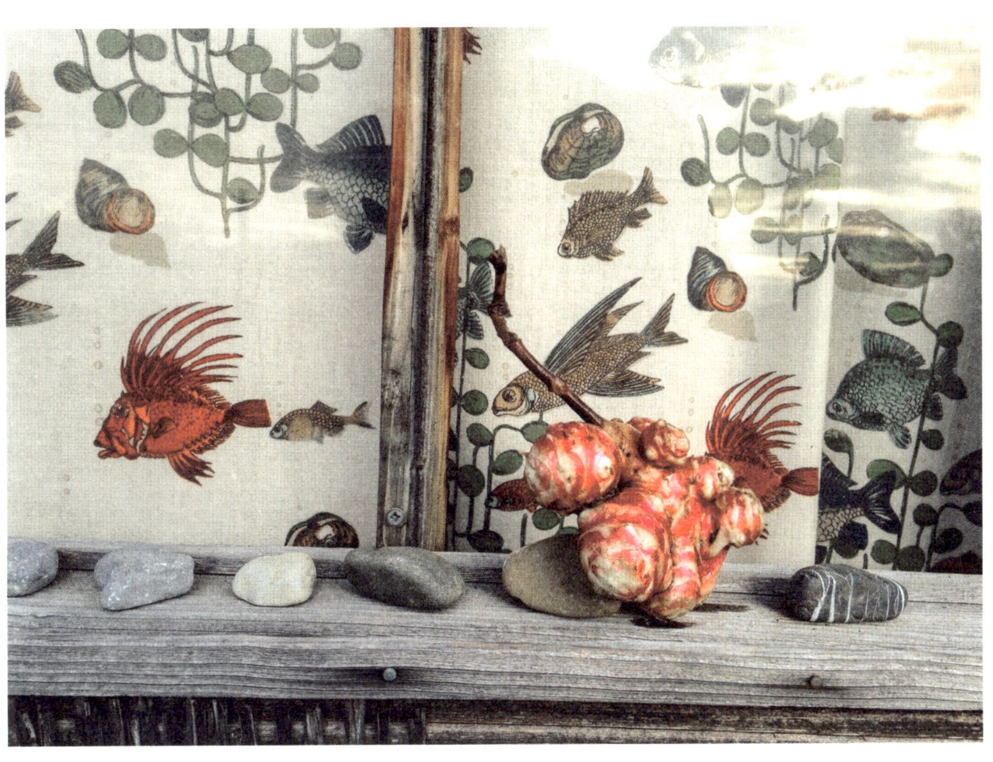

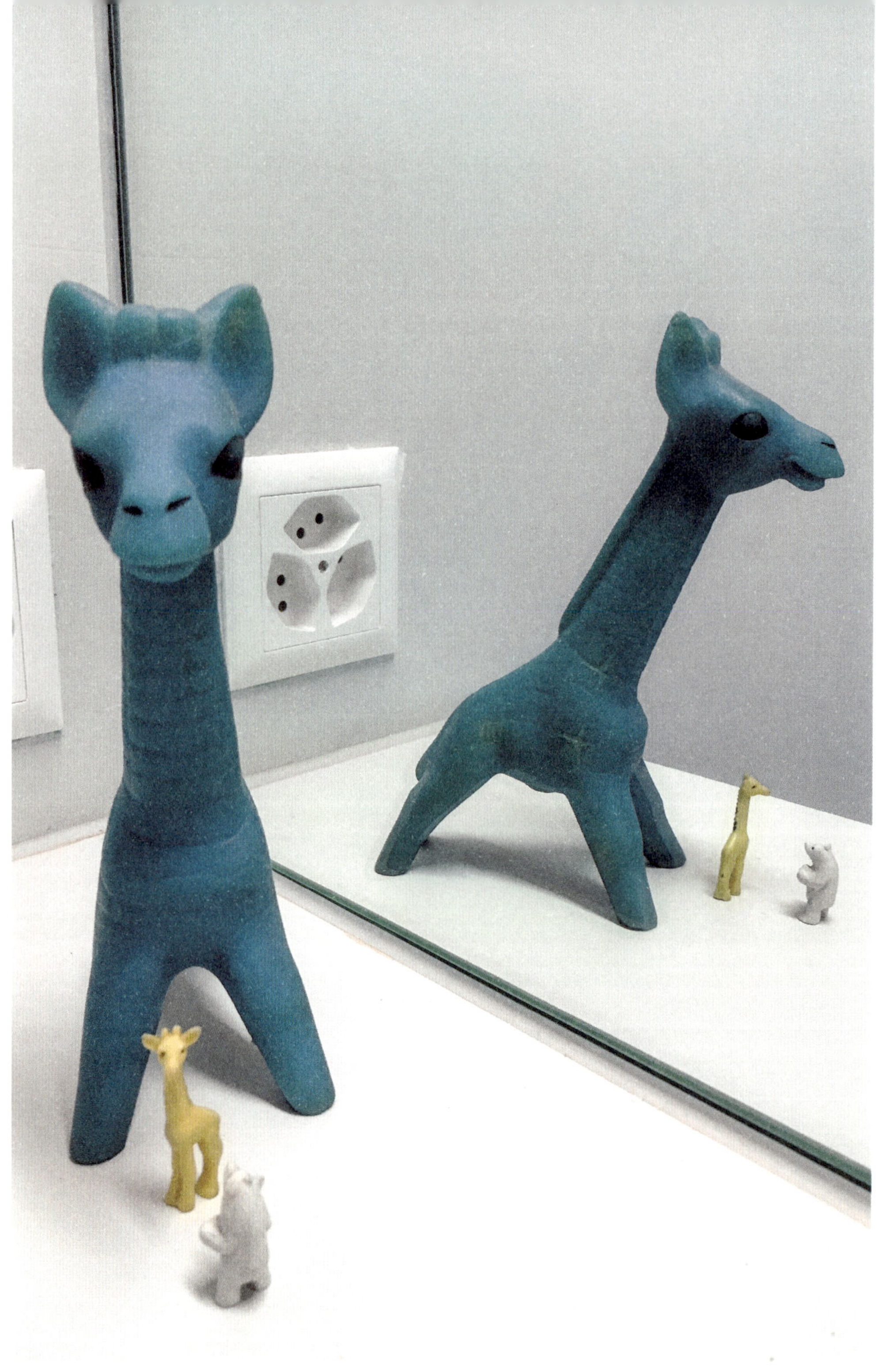

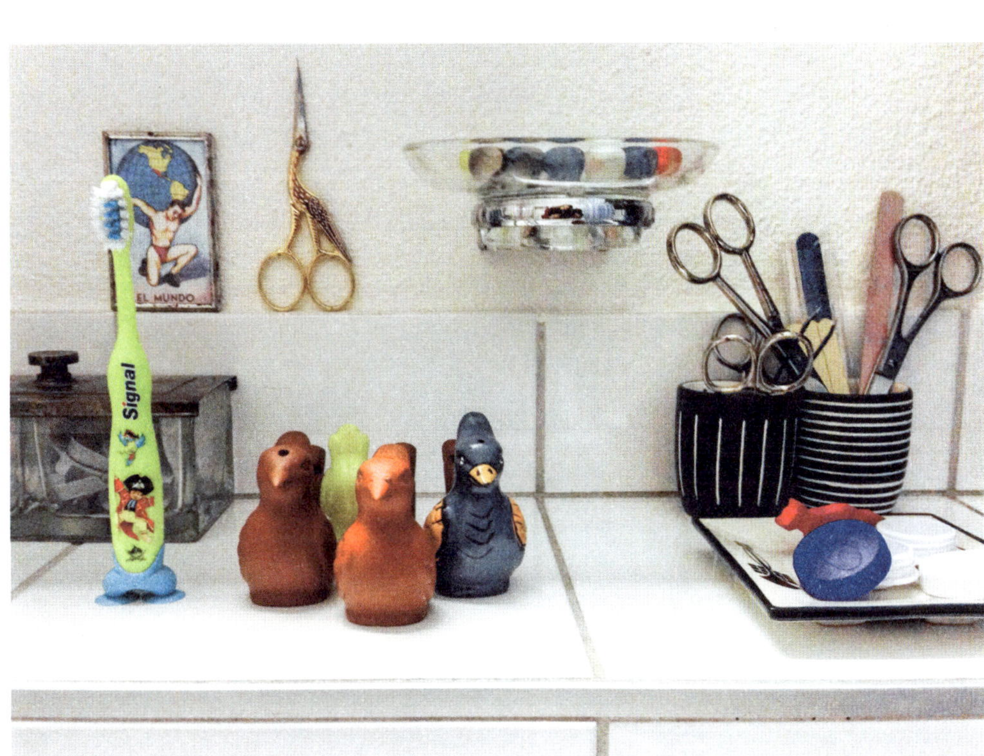

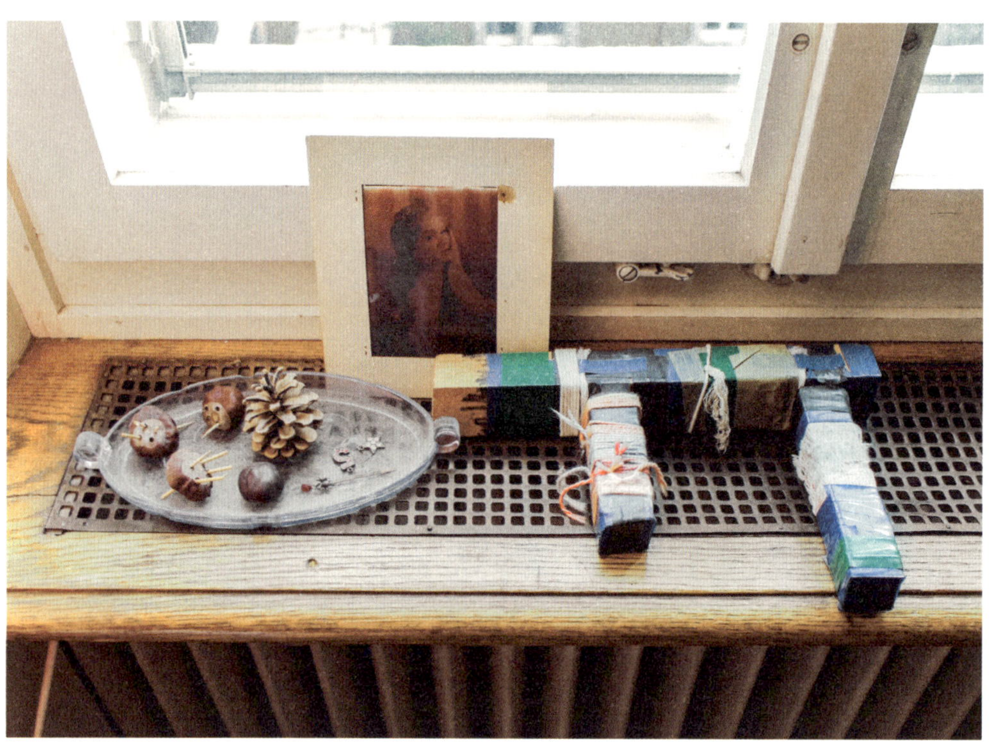

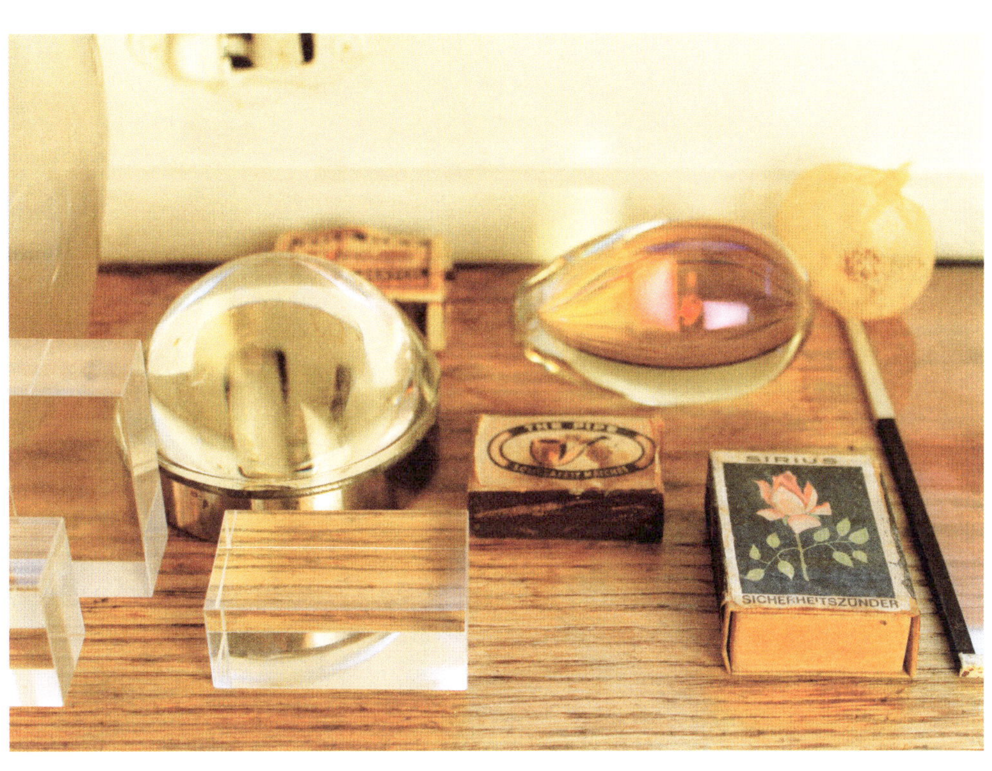
THE PIPE
SIRIUS
SICHERHEITSZÜNDER

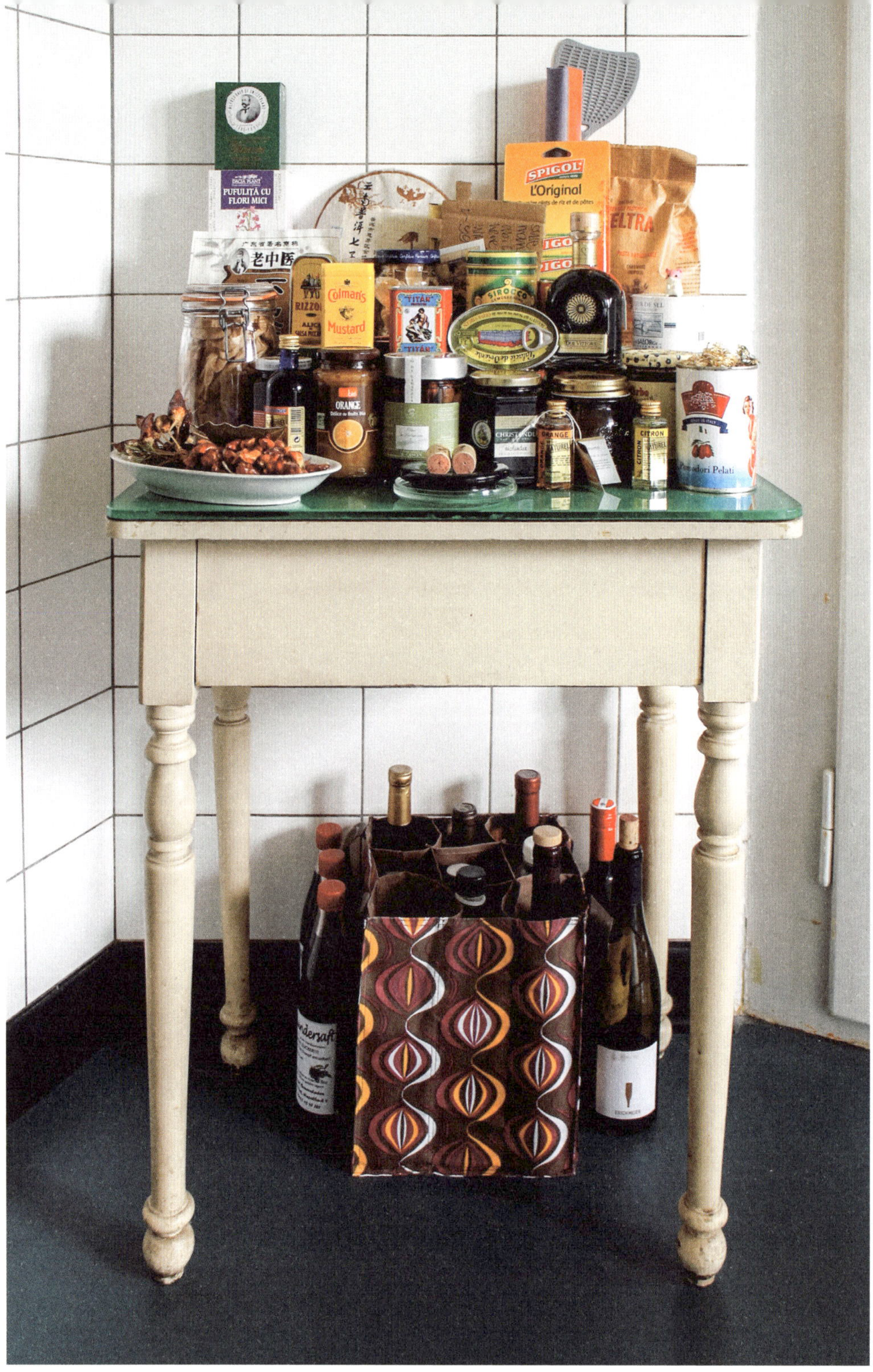

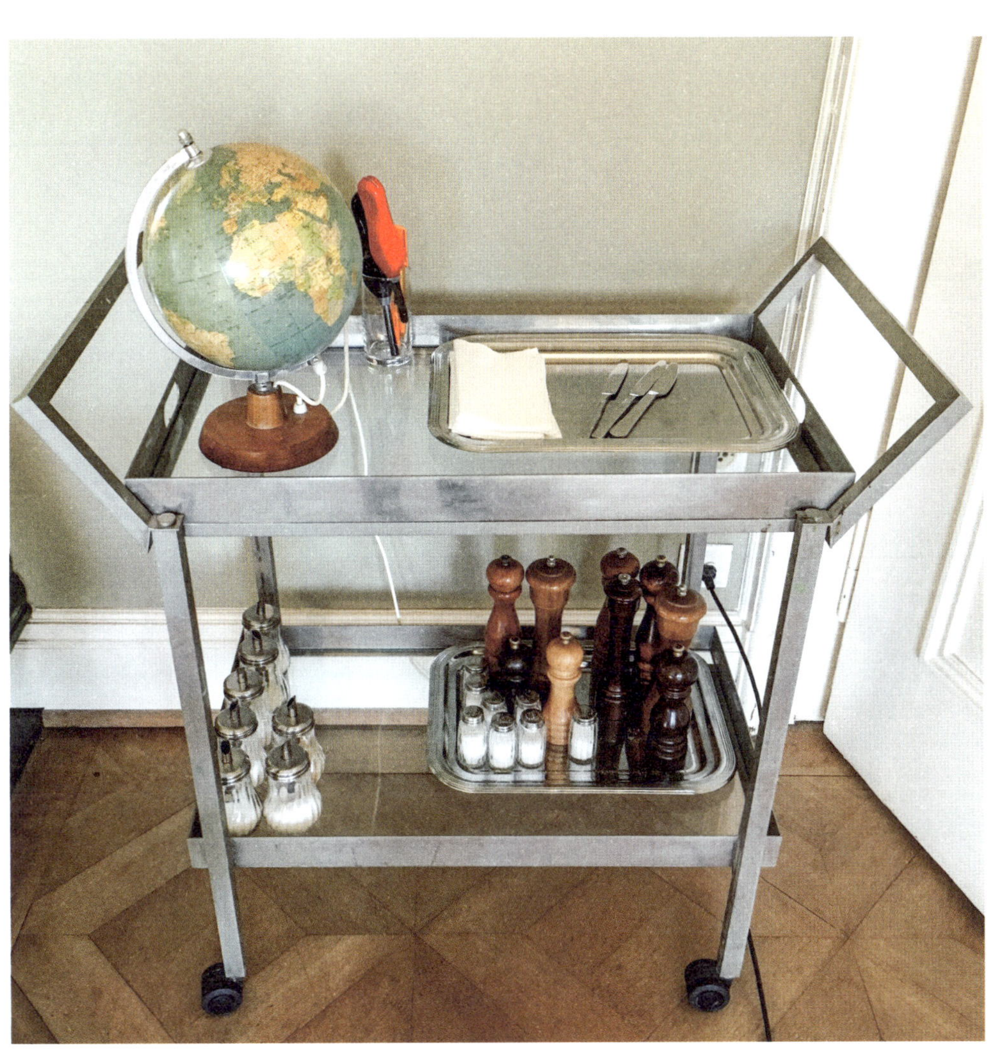

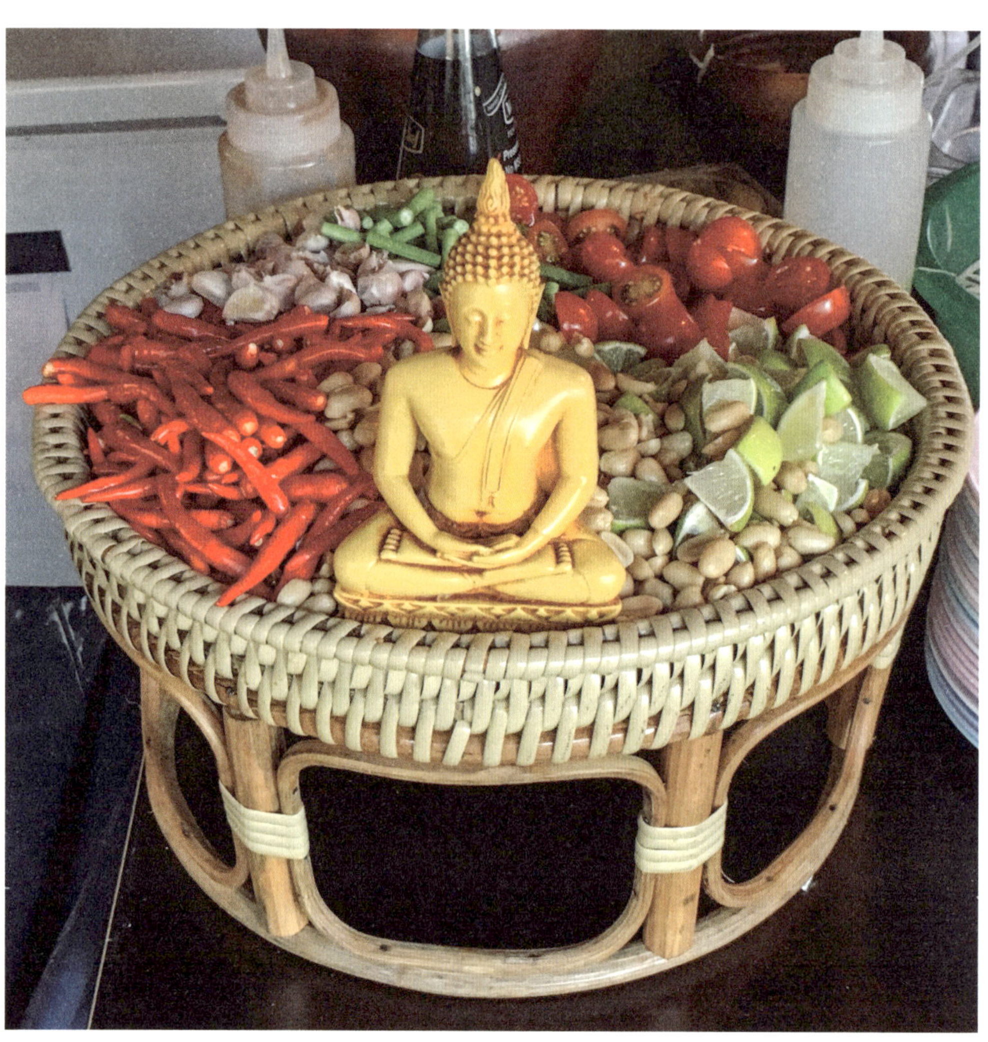

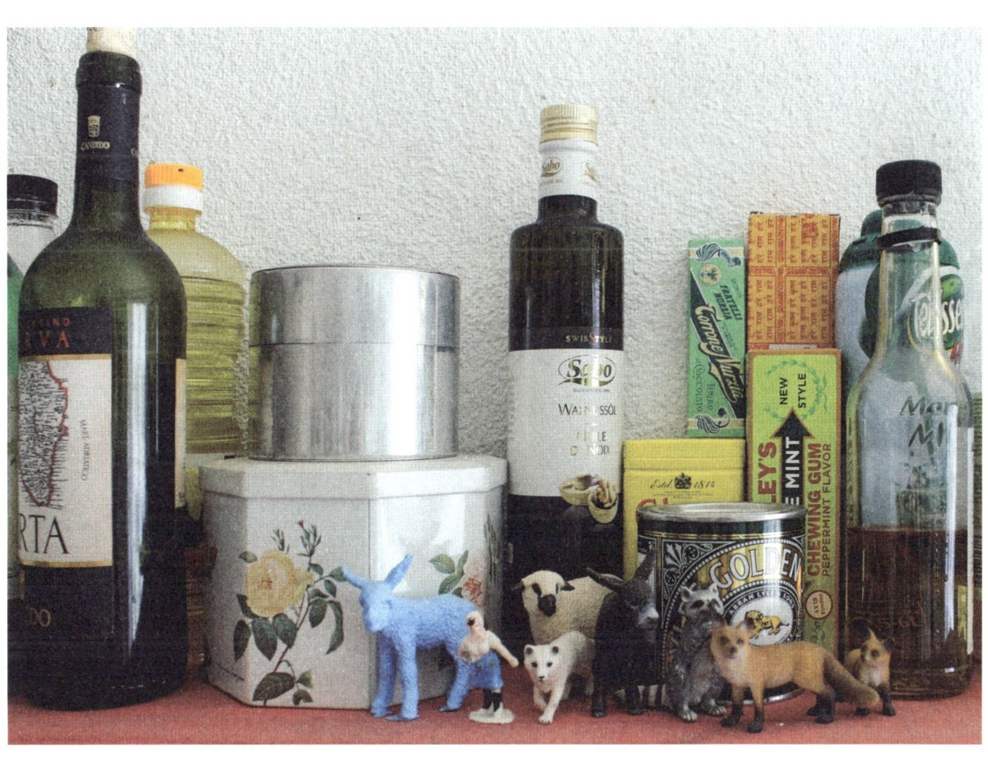

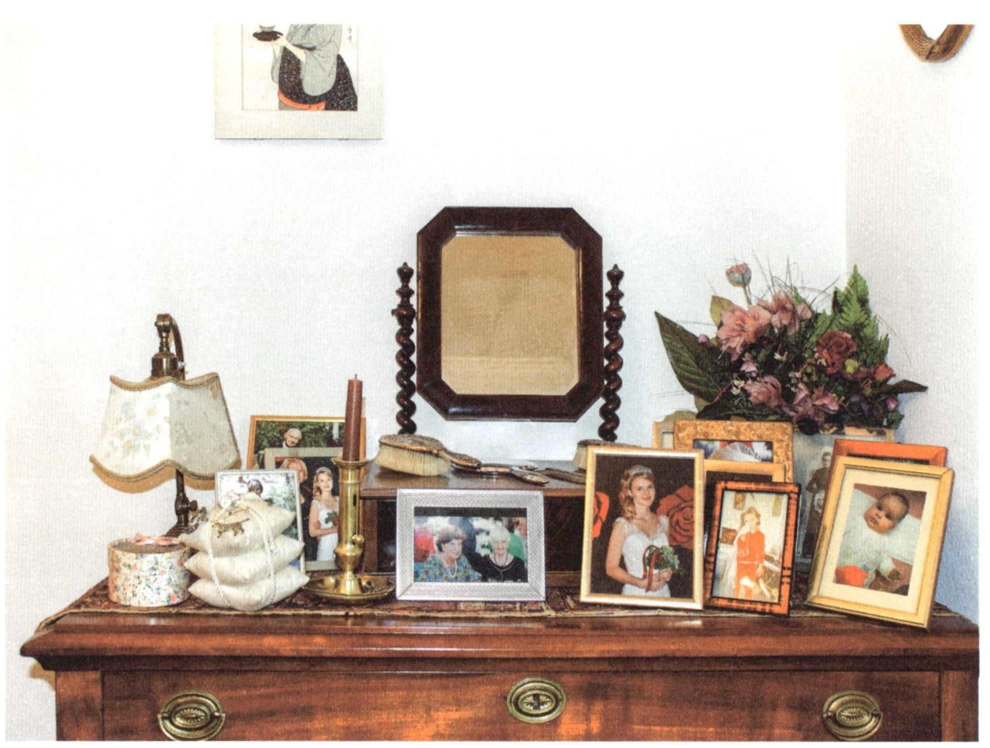

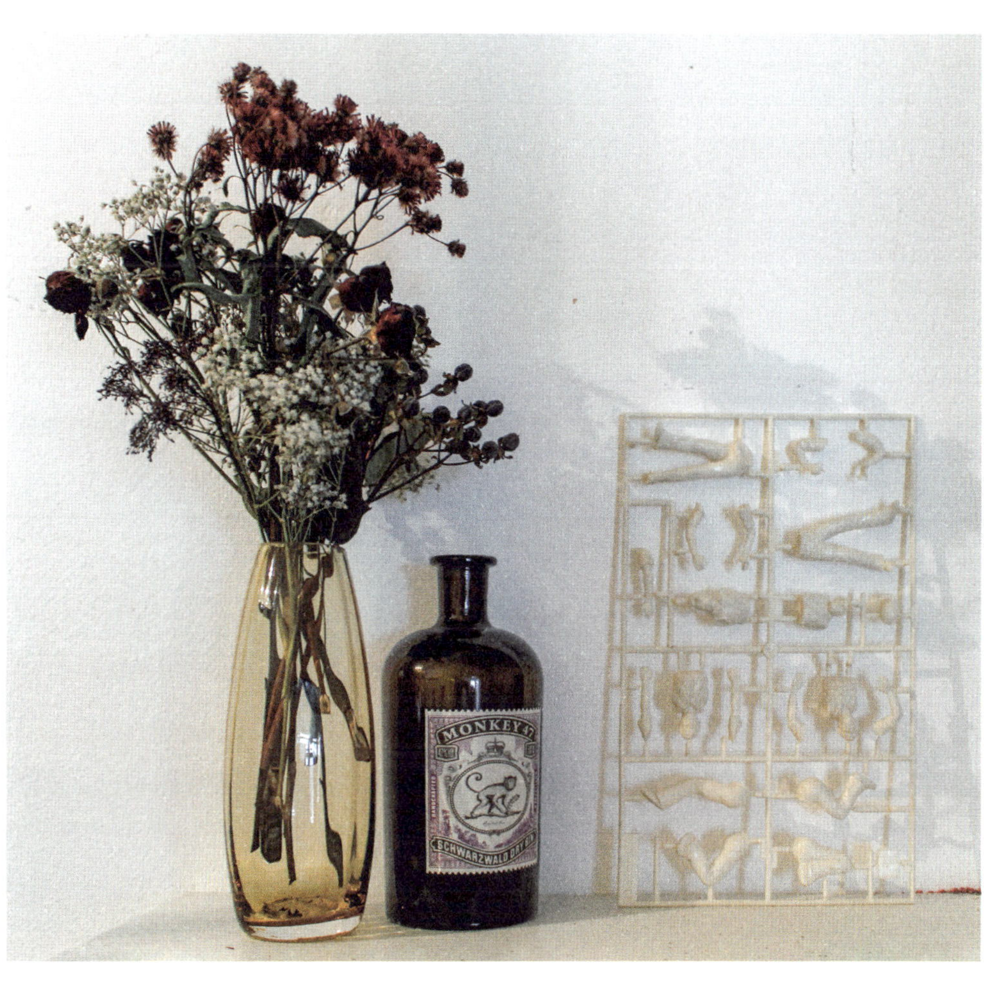

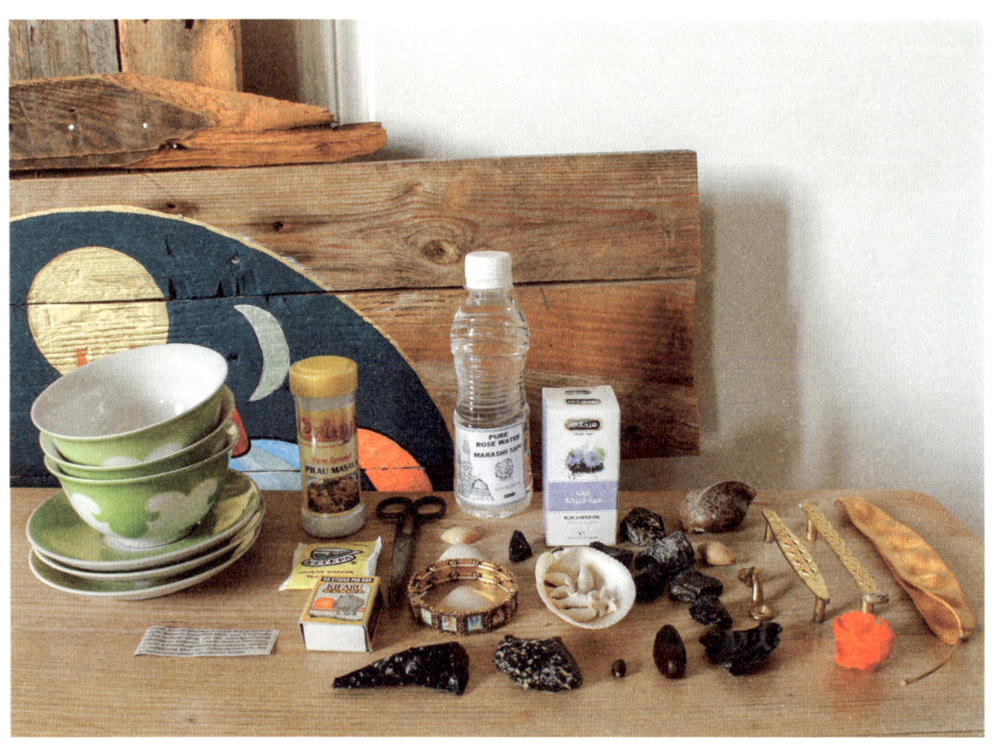

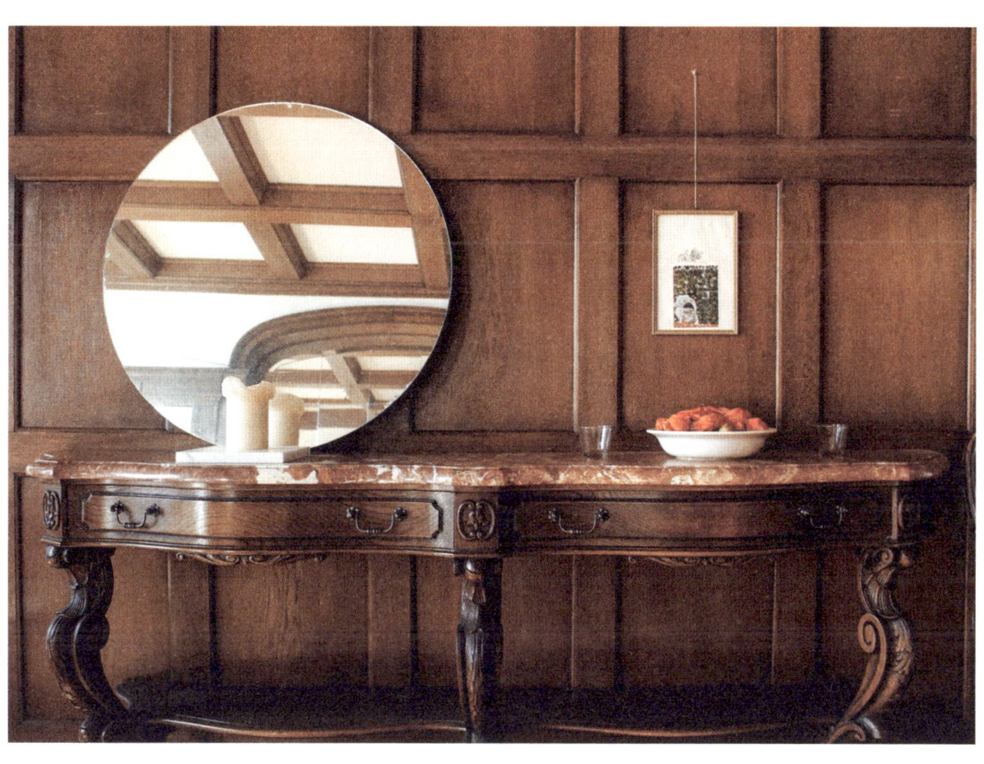

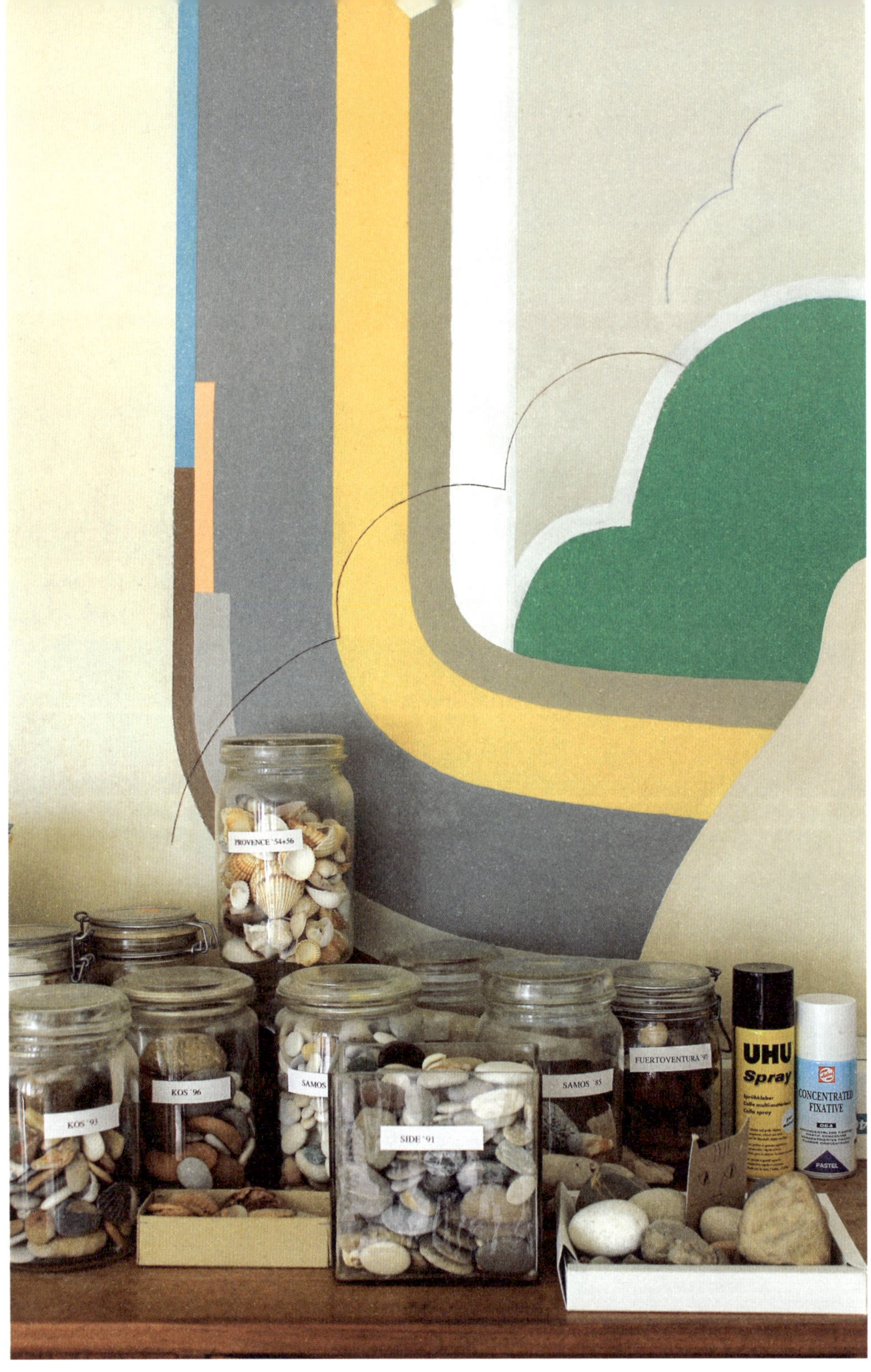

PROVENCE '54+56
KOS '93
KOS '96
SAMOS
SIDE '91
SAMOS '85
FUERTOVENTURA '97
UHU
Spray
Sprühkleber
Colle multi-matériaux
Colla spray
CONCENTRATED
FIXATIVE
PASTEL

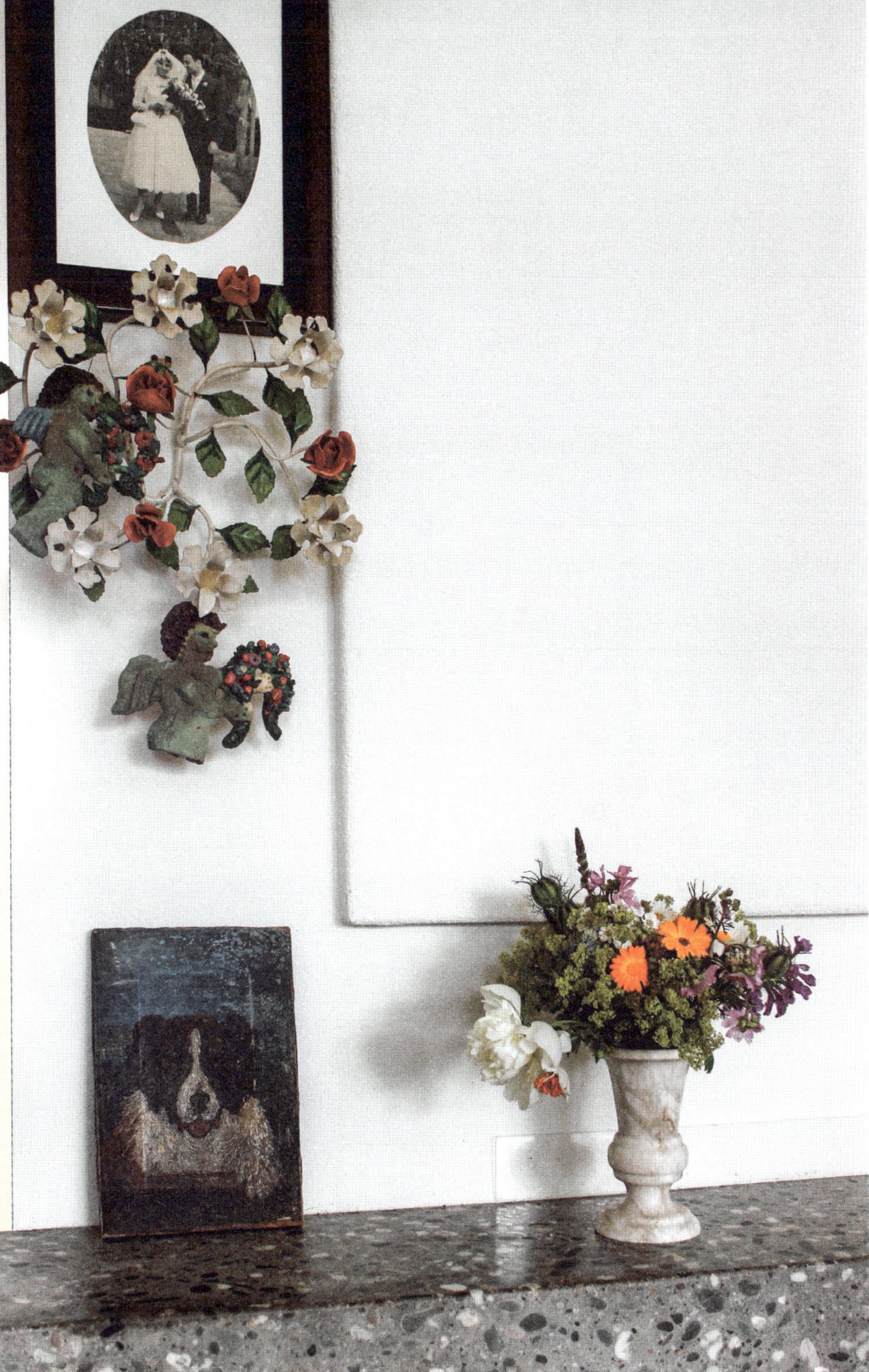

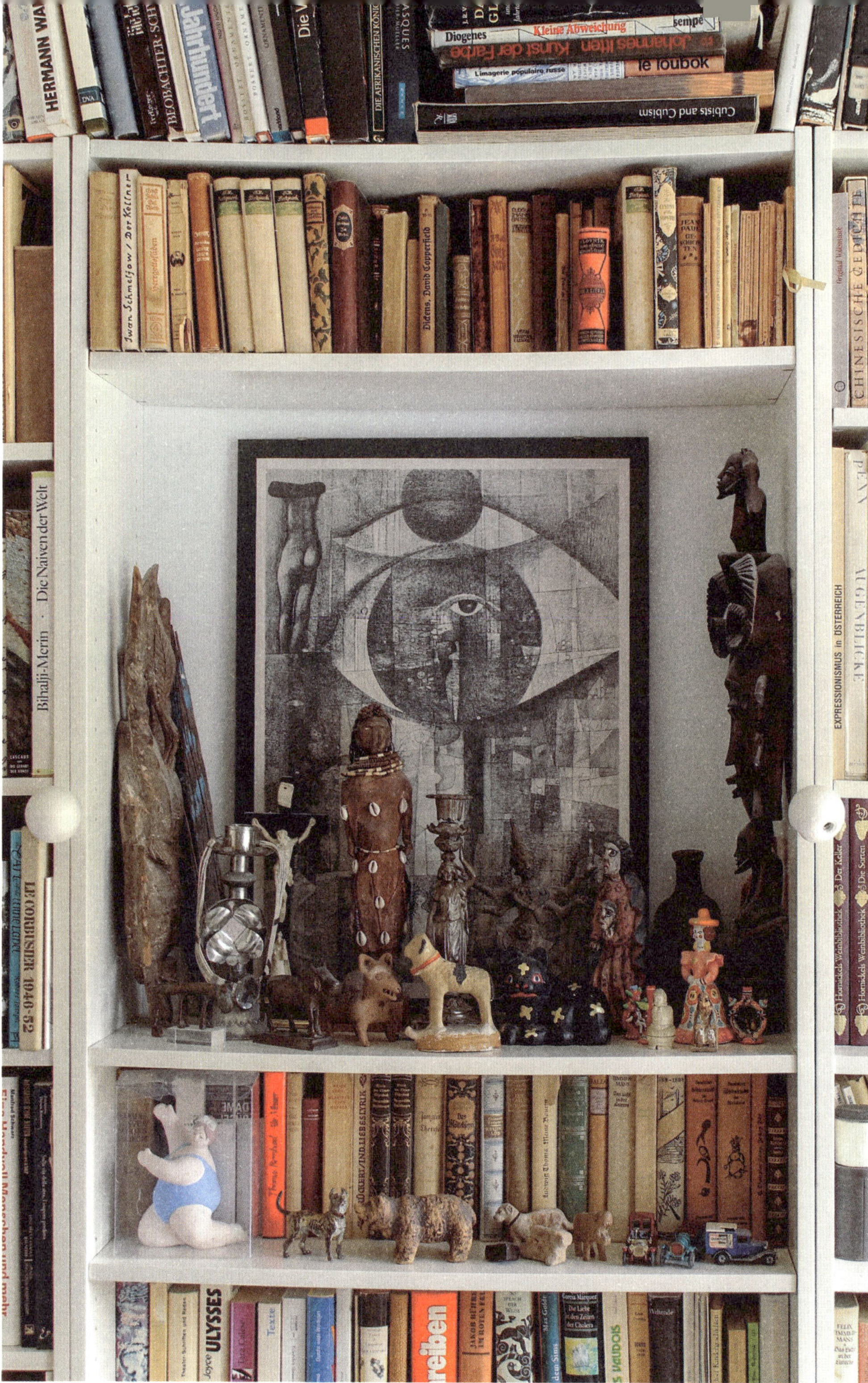

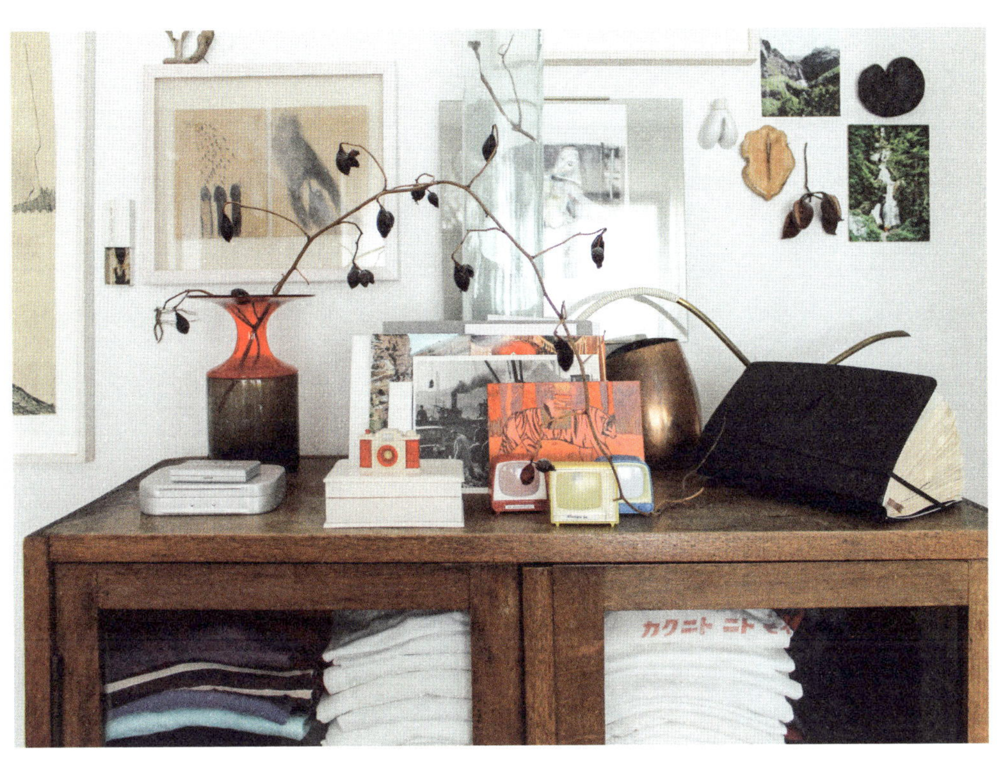

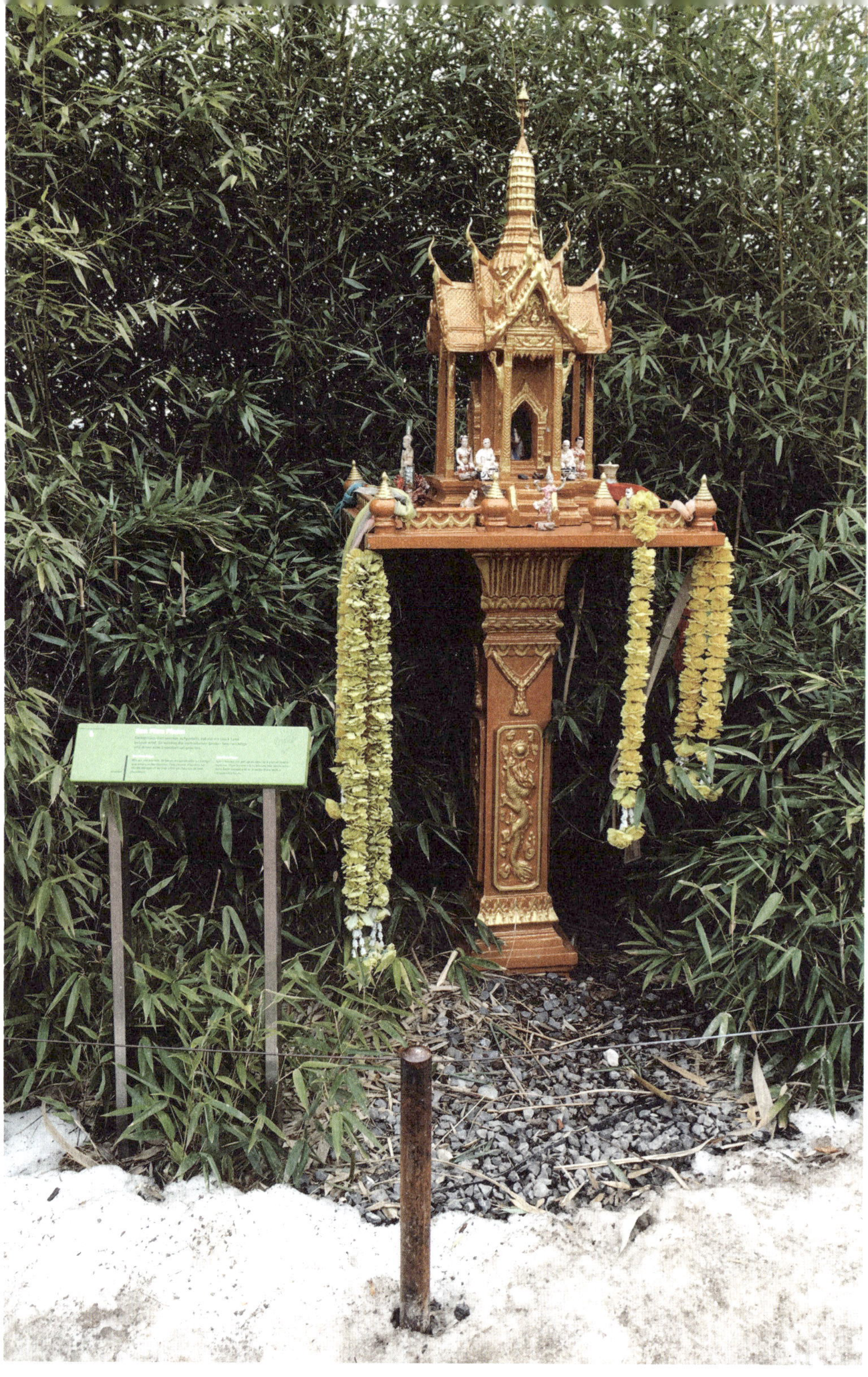

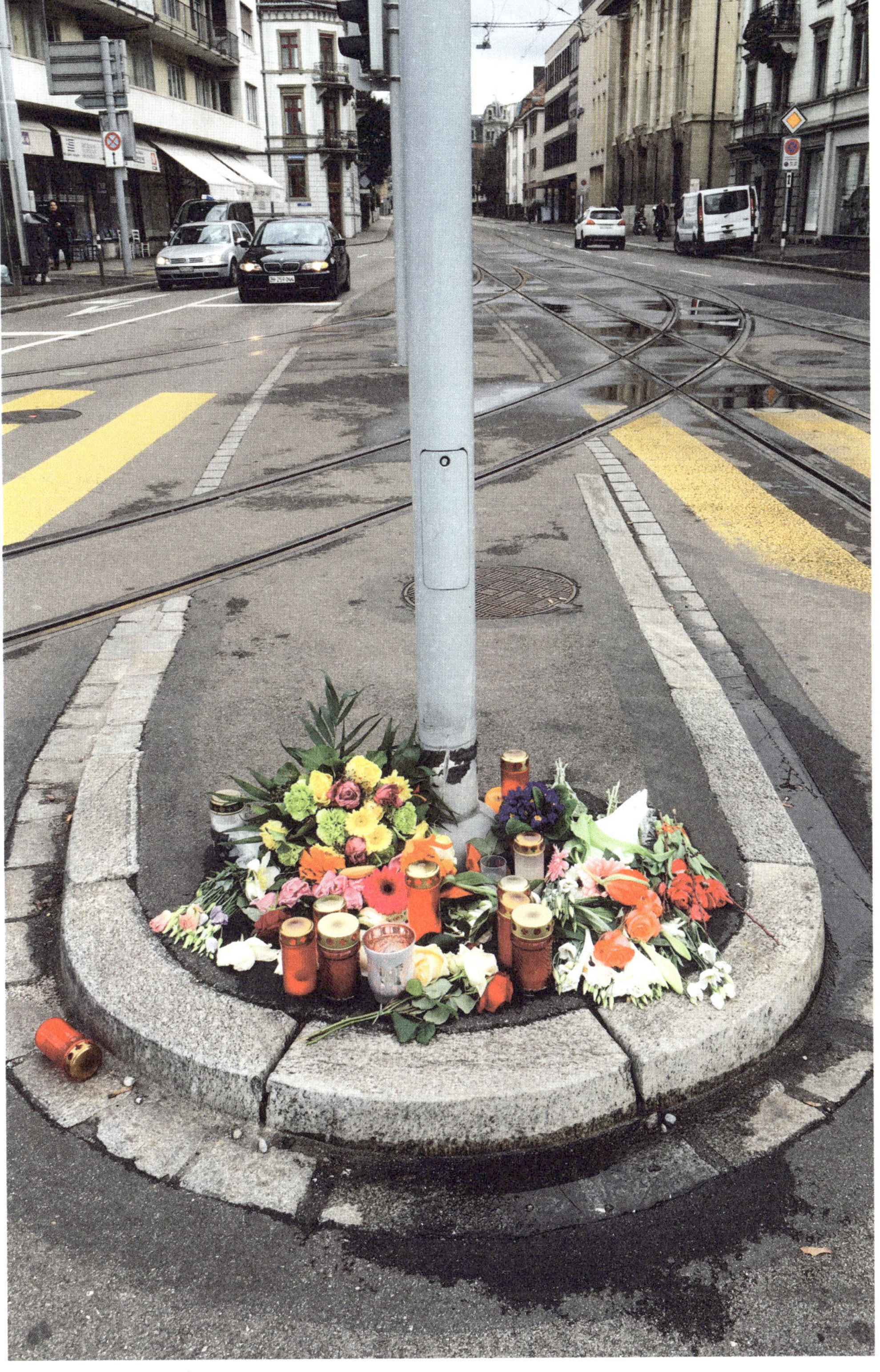

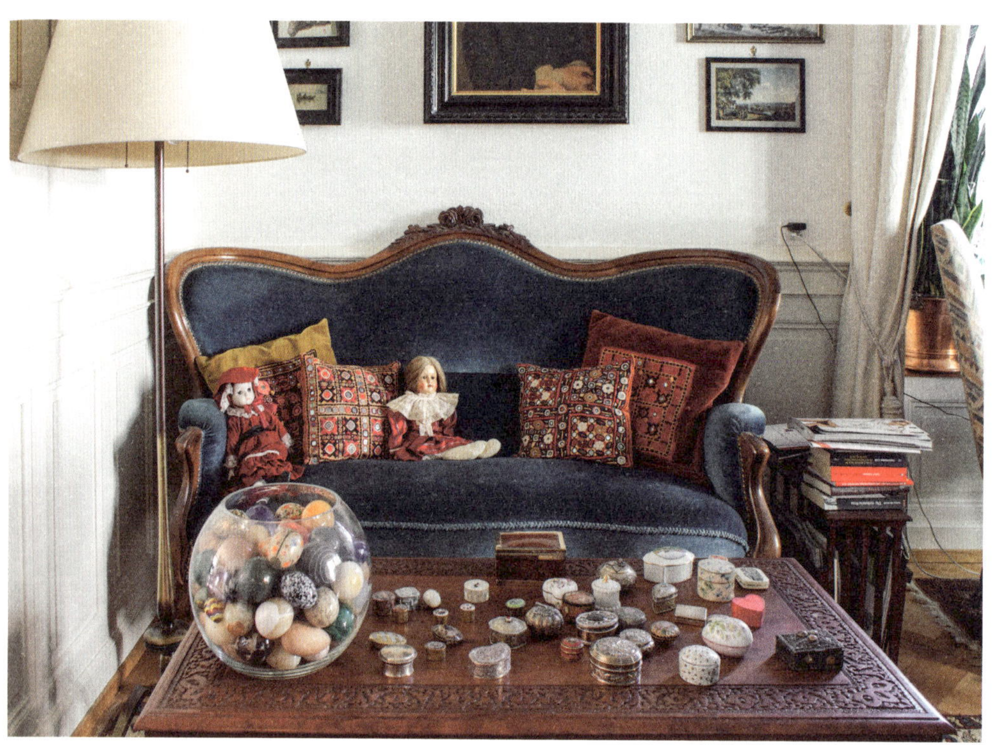

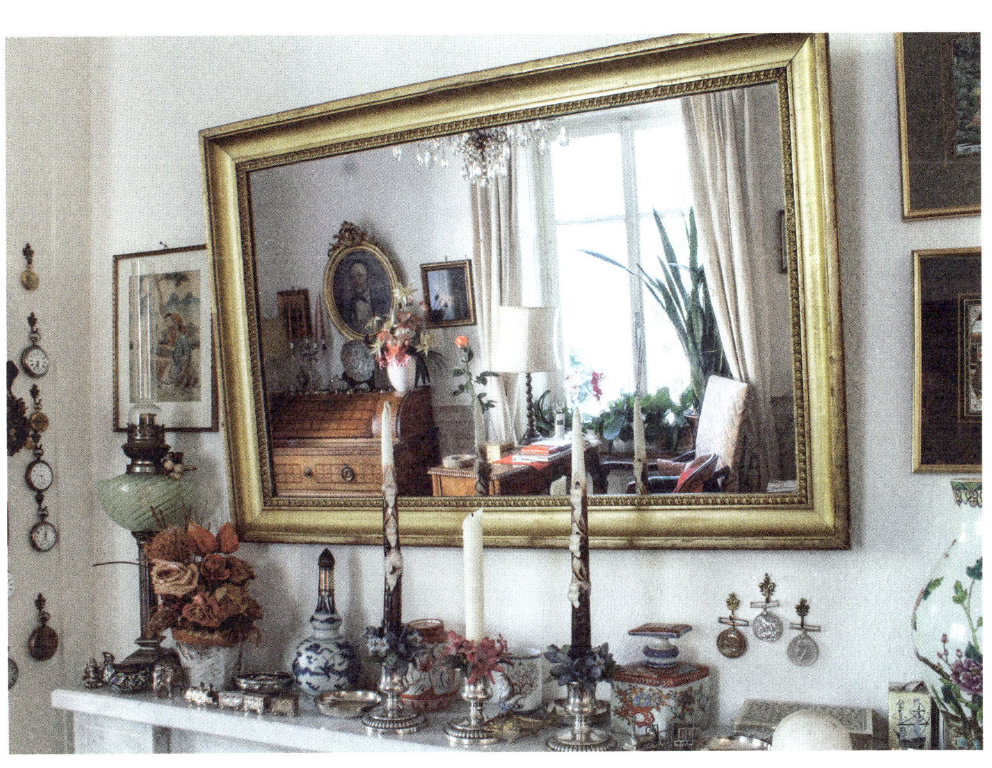

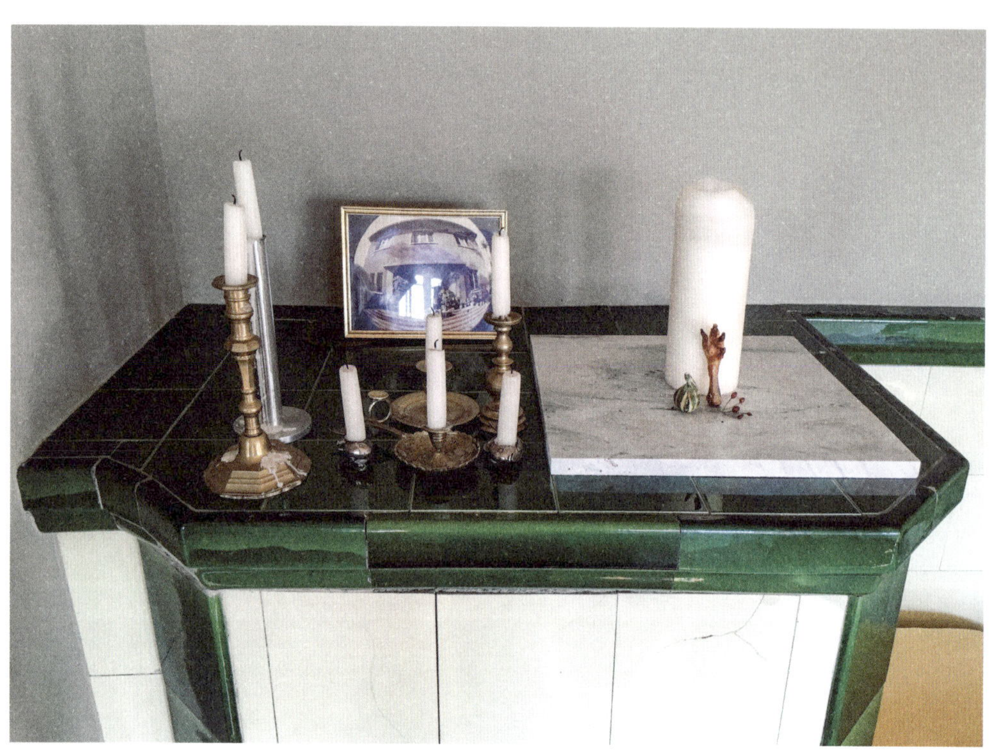

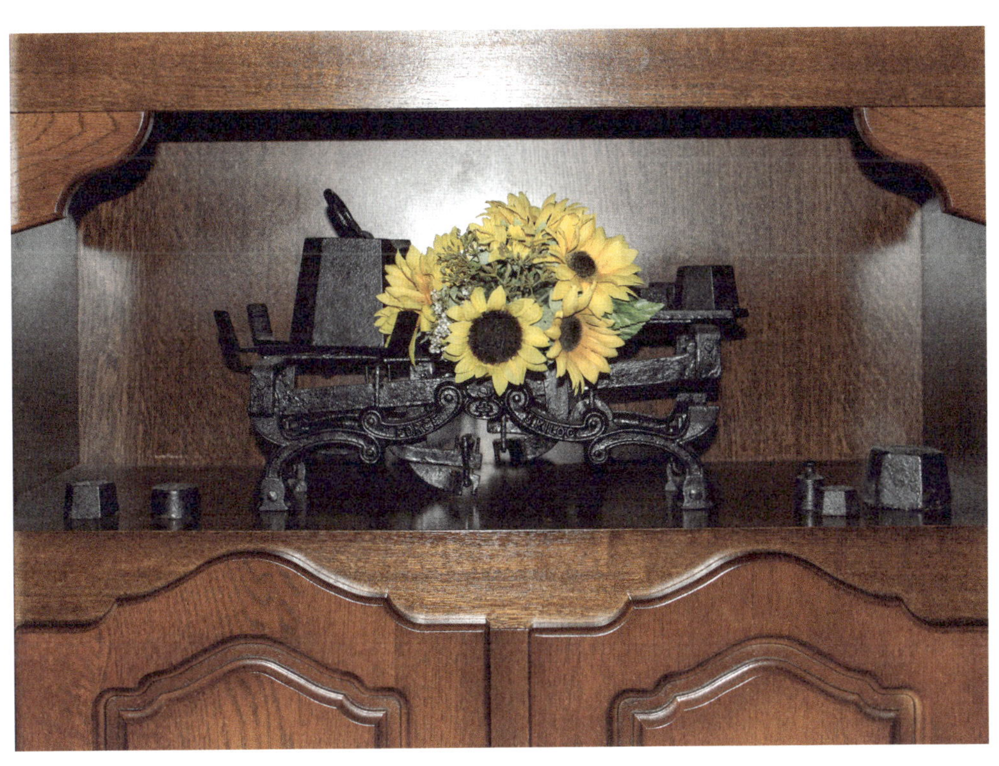

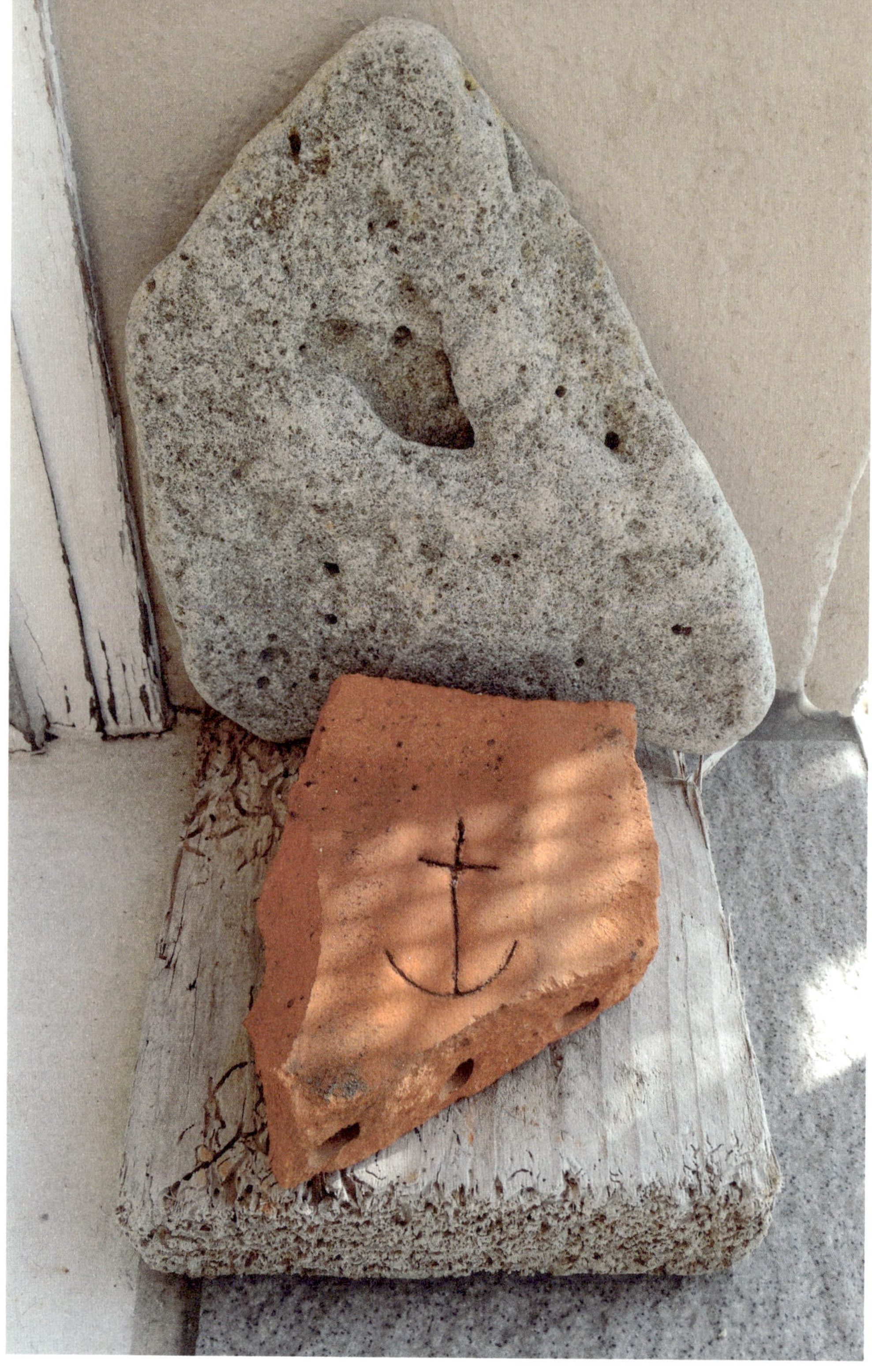

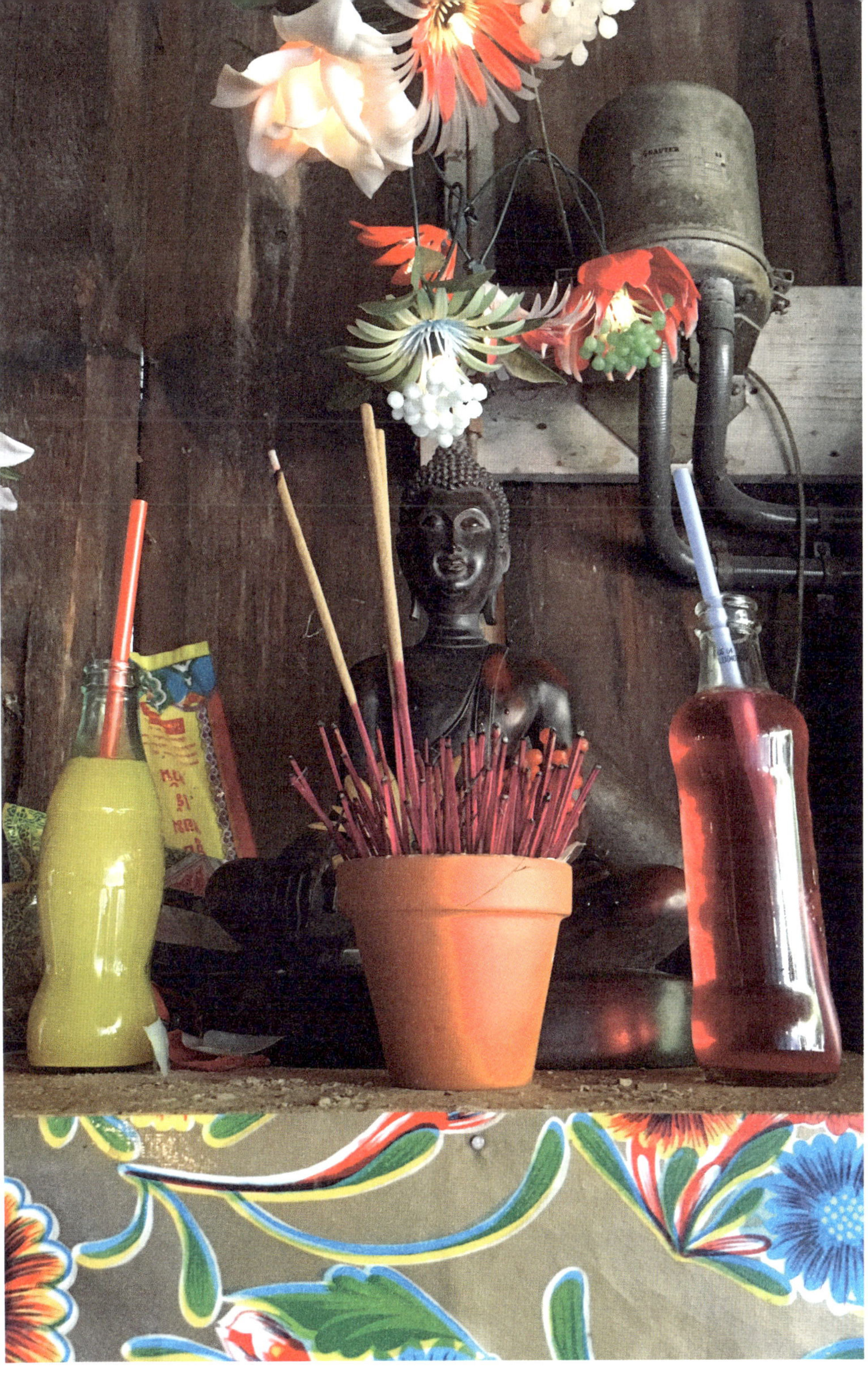

COLOPHON
Peter Schneider, Rosa Schamal, Manuel Süess
ALTAR

Text: Peter Schneider
Translations: Andreas Koller (German), Eric Rosencrantz (English)
Copyediting and proofreading:
Eric Rosencrantz (English), Miriam Wiesel (German)

Photo credits: Rosa Schamal

Book design: Manuel Süess
Printed and bound by DZA Druckerei zu Altenburg, Altenburg (DE)
Paper for text / photographs (incl. grammage): MunkenPolar 130 g/qm
Cover: 165 g/qm Iris Leinen. Canosa 605 ladybird
Font: CGP2000, AK12

First edition: Edition Patrick Frey, 2018
Print run: 700 copies
ISBN 978-3-906803-64-7
Printed in Germany

© 2018 photographs: the author
© 2018 text: the author
© 2018 for this edition: Edition Patrick Frey

Edition Patrick Frey, Limmatstrasse 268, CH-8005 Zürich
www.editionpatrickfrey.com
mail@editionpatrickfrey.ch

Rosa thanks: Patrick, Vera, Cäcilia, Nando, Giorgio, Barbara,
Georg, Martin, Heini, Christa, Manuel, the house with no name,
the things we love.

Distribution
Switzerland:
AVA Verlagsauslieferung, CH – Affoltern am Albis
ava.ch

Germany, Austria:
GVA Gemeinsame Verlagsauslieferung, D – Göttingen
gva-verlage.de

France, Luxembourg, Belgium:
Les presses du réel, F – Dijon
lespressesdureel.com

United Kingdom:
Antenne Books, GB – London
antennebooks.com

United States:
RAM publications + distribution, USA – Santa Monica
rampub.com

Japan:
twelvebooks, JP – Tokyo
twelve-books.com

Australia, New Zealand:
Perimeter Distribution, AU – Melbourne
perimeterdistribution.com

Rest of the world:
Edition Patrick Frey, CH – Zürich
editionpatrickfrey.com